P

HOW TO PRAY FOR HEALING

Pastor Ché Ahn digs down and finds answers that others have not uncovered to questions about healing. We are on the verge of a great wave of supernatural healing, and *How to Pray for Healing* will be one of the best resources we can draw upon to see a release of God's healing power.

CINDY JACOBS

AUTHOR, *THE VOICE OF GOD*

"I die a thousand deaths each time I walk out on stage," said the late Kathryn Kuhlman. Miss Kuhlman wasn't alone. We too may face the prospect of multitudes of needy, often desperate, people we can meet on the stage of private life and the stage of public ministry. Even those used of God in legendary ways in the capacity of healing have faced unanswered questions while seeking to help others in biblical response to their deep human needs. Ché Ahn has asked some of those questions during his journey with Christ since his conversion and dramatic calling into this ministry. *How to Pray for Healing* gives some pointed and practical answers that will go a long way to helping us come to grips with the command of Jesus: "As you go, . . . heal the sick" (Matt. 10:7-8).

WINKIE PRATNEY

AUTHOR, *REVIVAL* AND *FIRE ON THE HORIZON*
EVANGELIST

One of the great questions asked by many Christians is, Why do some people get healed and some don't? It is a good question. Jesus told His disciples to "keep on asking," "keep on seeking" and "keep on knocking." Those who did would receive, find and have the door opened. He taught almost desperate perseverance. If you need healing, I believe you will be strengthened in your faith as you read Ché Ahn's book *How to Pray for Healing.*

DR. PAT ROBERTSON

CHAIRMAN AND CEO, THE CHRISTIAN BROADCASTING NETWORK, INC.

While traveling around the country during the last few years, I've seen the need for believers and unbelievers alike to experience the healing power of the living God. Ché Ahn does more than give us a fresh look at healing—*How to Pray for Healing* imparts a *passion* to ask God to pour out His love into this hurting world. Read it, practice it, and watch God move.

DUTCH SHEETS

AUTHOR, *INTERCESSORY PRAYER*
PASTOR, SPRINGS HARVEST FELLOWSHIP
COLORADO SPRINGS, COLORADO

Few things today are more controversial in the Church than the issue of divine healing. In *How to Pray for Healing*, Ché Ahn removes the confusion and peels away the veneer regarding this critical issue. In a simple and transparent way, he provides us with a biblical foundation on which to base our faith.

ALICE SMITH

AUTHOR, *SPIRITUAL HOUSECLEANING*
U.S. PRAYER CENTER

HOW TO PRAY
FOR
HEALING

CHÉ AHN

Regal

From Gospel Light
Ventura, California, U.S.A.

PUBLISHED BY REGAL BOOKS
FROM GOSPEL LIGHT
VENTURA, CALIFORNIA, U.S.A.
PRINTED IN THE U.S.A.

Regal Books is a ministry of Gospel Light, an evangelical Christian publisher dedicated to serving the local church. We believe God's vision for Gospel Light is to provide church leaders with biblical, user-friendly materials that will help them evangelize, disciple and minister to children, youth and families.

It is our prayer that this Regal book will help you discover biblical truth for your own life and help you meet the needs of others. May God richly bless you.

For a free catalog of resources from Regal Books/Gospel Light, please call your Christian supplier or contact us at 1-800-4-GOSPEL or www.regalbooks.com.

All Scripture quotations, unless otherwise indicated, are taken from the *Holy Bible, New International Version®*. Copyright © 1973, 1978, 1984 by International Bible Society. Used by permission of Zondervan Publishing House. All rights reserved.

Other versions used are
NASB—Scripture taken from the NEW AMERICAN STANDARD BIBLE®, Copyright © 1960, 1962, 1963, 1968, 1971, 1972, 1973, 1975, 1977, 1995 by The Lockman Foundation. Used by permission.
NKJV—Scripture taken from the *New King James Version*. Copyright © 1979, 1980, 1982 by Thomas Nelson, Inc. Used by permission. All rights reserved.

© 2004 Ché Ahn
All rights reserved.

Cover design by Robert Williams
Interior design by Stephen Hahn
Edited by Steven Lawson

Library of Congress Cataloging-in-Publication Data

Ahn, Ché, 1956–
    How to pray for healing / Ché Ahn.
          p. cm.
Includes bibliographical references.
    ISBN 0-8307-3243-8
    1.   Spiritual healing.   2.   Prayer—Christianity.   I. Title.
    BT732.5.A35 2003
    234'.131—dc22   2003020769

1 2 3 4 5 6 7 8 9 10 11 12 13 14 15 / 09 08 07 06 05 04 03

Rights for publishing this book in other languages are contracted by Gospel Light Worldwide, the international nonprofit ministry of Gospel Light. Gospel Light Worldwide also provides publishing and technical assistance to international publishers dedicated to producing Sunday School and Vacation Bible School curricula and books in the languages of the world. For additional information, visit www.gospellightworldwide.org; write to Gospel Light Worldwide, P.O. Box 3875, Ventura, CA 93006; or send an e-mail to info@gospellightworldwide.org.

DEDICATION

This book is dedicated to
Young Sook Ahn
My mentor
My intercessor
My mother
1932-2002

CONTENTS

FOREWORD

Radical changes have begun in the Church. We have seen nothing like them since the days of the Protestant Reformation in the sixteenth century. What I like to call the New Apostolic Reformation began to take shape in American churches in the 1990s, and my best estimation is that the Second Apostolic Age itself began in 2001.

The reason I mention this is that the appearance of this book, *How to Pray for Healing*, comes at a perfect time. It is no accident that it is being released in the early years of the Second Apostolic Age. When Ché Ahn decided to write this book, he was definitely hearing what the Spirit is saying to the churches.

Ché Ahn is superbly qualified to produce this simple, straightforward, biblical, practical manual for every believer to use in his or her daily course of life. I have known Ché Ahn for a long time. In fact, years ago I had the privilege of helping to guide him through his master of divinity and doctorate of ministry degree programs at Fuller Theological Seminary. Ché has developed into one of the outstanding apostles of our time. Not only does he pastor Harvest Rock Church in Pasadena, California, and not only was he, along with Lou Engle, the leader of the notable youth movement The Call; but he is also the apostle over Harvest International Ministries (HIM), an apostolic network embracing more than 1,100 churches located in many parts of the world.

Many people would agree that the weakest area in the American version of the New Apostolic Reformation is evangelism. In terms of reaching the lost, we are lagging far behind dynamic moves of God in places such as Nigeria, China,

Indonesia, Nepal and Brazil. What is it that believers in these nations have that American believers don't have? Sadly enough, it is simple faith in the power of God.

Bible-believing Christians certainly acknowledge that God is all-powerful. They use, without hesitation, the theological term "omnipotent" when describing God. However, we in America sometimes have a difficult time bringing a practical application of this belief into our daily lives. Even in life-giving churches, the great majority of members rarely, if ever, see sick people instantly healed when they pray for them. Even less frequently do they cast out demons and raise the dead, as Jesus said His disciples did (see Mark 16:17-18).

This lack of signs and wonders is about to change. For a century, God has been bringing waves of divine prodding to encourage believers to practice power ministries. These waves began with the Pentecostal movement in the early 1900s and continued with the healing evangelists after World War II, the charismatic renewal in the 1960s, the Third Wave in the 1980s and finally the outpourings such as the Toronto Blessing, the Brownsville revival and others.

Unfortunately, none of the above movements produced the widespread shift in the entire Body of Christ that many Christians had expected. In my opinion, this could have been due largely to the fact that back then the gifts and offices of apostle and prophet had not been widely recognized. However, the Second Apostolic Age has changed the picture. The foundation of the Church, namely apostles and prophets (see Eph. 2:20), is now in place—at least initially.

We are now moving into the day of the saints (to use a phrase popularized by Bill Hamon of Christian International Ministries Network). This means that you and I are about to see things happen that neither we nor our parents have seen.

God is going to move so strongly throughout the Church that the ordinary people in the pews will surprise themselves with how many unbelievers they lead to Christ through supernatural signs and wonders. The saints movement is not something that we can produce by our sheer willpower or by following a series of prescribed steps. God Himself is going to do it.

Are you ready? When this begins, you will want to be as prepared as you can be. That's why this book is so important. Praying for the sick can be a bit uncomfortable if you are not familiar with the basic principles. In this book, Ché Ahn will introduce you to some basic principles in a very understandable way. You will be excited as you experience the power of God flowing through you so strongly that the sick people whom you pray for will actually get well.

Not only will you love this book, but you will also probably want to pick up a few copies for your friends.

C. Peter Wagner
Chancellor, Wagner Leadership Institute

ACKNOWLEDGMENTS

I want to thank those who helped me craft and edit this book. Thank you, Chung-Hae Casler, my beloved sister, and thank you, Stephanie Casler, my niece, for doing the first run of editing. I want to thank the awesome team at Regal Books: Bill Greig III, Kim Bangs, Kyle Duncan, Deena Davis, Steven Lawson and Stephanie Parrish. Thank you, Bill, for being my friend as well as my publisher and thank you for believing in me. Thank you, Steve, for your labor of love to flesh out and edit the book to really reflect what was on my heart. Thank you, Pat Robertson and Larry Tomczak, for adding meaningful appendixes to this book.

Above all, I want to thank my wonderful family: Sue—my best friend and wife—and Gabriel, Grace, Joy and Mary—my amazing godly children. Thank you for releasing me to run with The Call and thank you for supporting me with this book.

Finally, I want to thank my Lord Jesus Christ who has been so loving and gracious to me. To You be all glory, honor and praise.

Introduction

A GREAT MYSTERY

I've never written a book on the how and why of divine healing—even though I've been besieged with requests to do so—simply because I don't know the how and why.

KATHRYN KUHLMAN, *KATHRYN KUHLMAN: THE WOMAN WHO BELIEVES IN MIRACLES*

We all love mysteries. Give us an Agatha Christie whodunit or a James Patterson brainteaser, and we want to solve the crime. Give us a crossword puzzle, and we want to fill in the blanks. Give us a reality television show, and we want to guess who will survive another week. Whatever the puzzle, in the end, we want all of the pieces to fit together.

We often do this with God, too. He can at times be mysterious, yet we want to figure Him out and define His actions. We yearn for concrete answers—usually on our own terms, since it is difficult for us to fully fathom His flawlessness and our fragility, His rock-solid grasp and our all-too-human gasps. We habitually attempt to stuff Him into our finite boxes—even though we know He is infinite. We want more, but we see in a mirror dimly (see 1 Cor. 13:12) and can perceive only a piece of God's bigger picture. As imperfect beings standing before a perfect God, we must resolve to simply trust and obey. Amazingly, when we do, the pieces begin to fit together and our faith grows.

When it comes to physical healing, we know that we need to walk in the same faith we apply to other areas of life. But it is not as easy. Instead, we tend to strive even harder for tangible explanations. We are not satisfied knowing that God can fix our bodies; we want to know how and why—and why He sometimes delays His answer. Some of us even want to see the miracle with our own eyes or at least have documented medical proof. It's curious how we can put more credence in a note from a doctor than a touch from God.

I am not suggesting we shrug off the questions; rather, I propose that we take a fresh look at healing. Too often we spend more time asking questions and not enough time following God's instructions.

I have been in the healing ministry for nearly 30 years. God has healed me, my family, my friends and countless people for whom I have prayed. He often gives me specific information about a person's need and bolsters my faith to believe for the impossible. Usually, after praying, I just stand back in awe, a witness to His miraculous power. I have seen both small and large ailments mended. In this book, I recount some of my experiences, and I hope they will strengthen your faith, too.

Despite undeniable and extraordinary results, I nonetheless am like the late healing evangelist Kathryn Kuhlman in that I do not pretend to know the how and why. There are seven octillion (7,000,000,000,000,000,000,000,000,000) atoms in the average adult body. How can God sort them all out, let alone fix any of them? Why does healing sometimes come instantaneously, sometimes over time, sometimes through the hands of a doctor and sometimes not right now? It is a mystery.

Some Christians point to New Testament passages—especially in Matthew (see for example Matt. 4:24; 8:16)—that recount how Jesus healed everyone who came to Him and suggest that we should expect the same. They insist healing is there just for the asking, but they rarely grapple with the obvious: Not everyone is healed every time someone prays.

Other Christians explain that God does not always heal because we live in the "already and not yet." In other words, the kingdom of God is growing (it's already here) but is not yet in its fullness. These people argue that as we see more of the kingdom of God come to Earth, we will see an increase in healing, deliverance and miracles.

Still other believers choose not to think much about the issue. They contend that healing depends solely on the sovereignty of God. While these people believe God can heal, their frustration with not having all of the pieces of the puzzle often results in a lack of regular prayer and little expectation for the miraculous.

This can be quite confusing. How do we sort it all out? I would not for a second consider writing the last word on the subject. I am not an expert. Nonetheless, from Scripture we can glean insight. When it comes to healing, we may not know the how and why of God's ways, but we can know the how and why of what God expects from us.

In this book I unravel some of the muddled issues—including common misconceptions and stumbling blocks—that keep us from praying for healing for others or from accepting wholeness for ourselves. I write specifically about physical healing, but the Bible is replete with teaching on how God can redeem every aspect of our lives—starting with salvation for our souls. In fact, sometimes the greatest healing has nothing to do with a body part or organ; rather, it repairs the deepest places in our spirits and our relationship with God.

None of these facts diminish God's ability and desire to heal. In fact, when it comes to physical healing, I have learned that combining and applying certain biblical principles actually increase the potential for manifestation. The mystery remains, but more results are seen. In this book, I will walk through these basic biblical models. I hope that as more of us apply these elements, many people will be healed and many will be equipped to extend Jesus' healing touch to a hurting world.

Chapter 1

THE MOST
IMPORTANT FACTOR

Clearly in Jesus' thinking the spiritual reality that the healing
pointed to—forgiveness of sins and the progressive revelation
of Christ's messiahship—was more important than
the physical miracle itself.
JOHN WIMBER, *POWER HEALING*

I needed to be healed. I did not have cancer, diabetes or even a
toothache. My ears, nose, hands and feet all worked fine; yet I
was broken. I needed to be fixed deep inside, in a place no doctor could touch.

I tell my story not to glamorize the sin in which I once excelled but to open the window to my past to show how God heals, beginning with the most important part. Physical healing is great—thank God He does it—but the inner work, of which the cornerstone is salvation, is greater than any bodily healing, as the late Vineyard Ministries International leader John Wimber correctly points out. Let's keep this in mind as we begin our journey into the great mystery of God's healing touch and as we learn how to pray for the sick.

My Story: From Zen to Jesus

I really thought I had it all together. The year was 1973, and I was 17. I was popular, had a good-looking girlfriend and money—I was making more than $2,000 a month selling drugs (that went a long way back then!). The hippie movement was alive and well, and I was a part of it. Parties and hedonism were my passions. One high would lead to another. For a while, it was a blast; yet something was missing.

I tried to quiet myself, but there was something gnawing at me on the inside. I didn't recognize the stirring as God's trying to reach my heart, but I had a hunch it had something to do with religion. Christianity was not a possibility; I dismissed it out-of-hand, because it was the faith of my parents and a mainstay in the so-called establishment (this was not long after pop philosopher Abby Hoffman had advised all youth to never trust anyone over 30). I was the epitome of this maxim, and I refused to conform to society's norms. Therefore, when it came to religion, I turned to Zen Buddhism. Although I didn't study the Eastern religion in depth and only recall attending two meetings, I was given my mantra and chanted incessantly for nine months. Of course, I continued to party and sell drugs, too.

As I played out this internal tug-of-war to fill the vacuum within me, questions remained unanswered—in fact, they loomed larger than ever.

Running from God

At the time I did not recognize the voice of God calling me. I did, however, know how to raise my own voice, and I knew how to flee. One day, after my father and I had a heated verbal fight, I ran away from home. Not having any place in particular to go, I made my way to Northampton, Massachusetts, to see my older sister, a freshman at Smith College. Being a "good" sibling, she took me in and invited me to a fraternity party. I felt right at home with a small cluster of college students who were drinking alcohol and smoking pot. From my jacket pocket, I pulled out a one-pound bag of marijuana and shared it with the nearest hippie. For some reason, we started talking about religion. I explained how I was into Zen. Another student, who was also getting high, overheard us and opined, "Hey, Zen is not the answer. Jesus is the answer. Jesus loves you, man, and I love you!" I immediately felt uncomfortable. I didn't mind his telling me that Jesus loved me, but when he declared that *he* loved me, I honestly thought he was a homosexual and that he was coming on to me. I got up and left the party. As I walked away, the words "Jesus loves you" rang in my ears.

Crying Out for Help

Eventually I returned home to Rockville, Maryland, a town outside of Washington, D.C. My friends heard that I was back, so they invited me to a party. We drank beer, smoked pot and blasted rock-and-roll music. After about an hour, I grew tired of the party. I went into an adjacent bedroom, where I sat cross-legged on a bed and started to chant my Zen mantra. In the midst of my ritual, I realized that I had gotten absolutely nothing out of nine months of chanting. I was so disgusted that I stopped chanting the mantra on the spot.

> ## GOD CARES ABOUT MAKING EVERY PART OF US WHOLE: MIND, SPIRIT AND BODY.

"God!" I cried aloud in my anguish and frustration. "I don't even know if You exist. But if You *do* exist and what my parents told me is true, that Jesus died for my sins and that—if there is a heaven and a hell—You are the way to heaven, I want to know the truth. I don't want to go hell; I want to go to heaven! After all, if You're God and You're all powerful, can't You reveal Yourself to me?"

As soon as I said those words, the presence of God came on me. Of course, at the time I didn't know what was happening. Looking back, though, I realize that it was the Holy Spirit's manifest presence. Something like scales fell from my eyes (see Acts 9:18), and I was stunned to realize that Jesus Christ was the answer I had been seeking all of my life. I thought to myself, *All this time the answer for humanity was right in front of me—revealed by my parents' beliefs—and I was looking for the answer in drugs, sex and Zen.*

God's presence and the revelation that Jesus Christ is the way, the truth and the life affected me so greatly that I started to weep. I literally felt His love. What amazed me was that I *knew* I was a rebel and a very selfish person, yet He still revealed Himself to me. Even though I didn't fully understand everything about God, let alone exactly what had transpired, in my heart I promised, *If this is the kind of God You are, then I'm in. I will follow You no matter what.*

After regaining some composure, I returned to the other room where the party was still blasting away. I blurted out to my friends, "Hey, man, I found what we're all looking for! I found the truth. I found Jesus!" They became very quiet and concerned. They thought I had taken one toke too many or was completely flipped out on drugs. In reality, it was just the opposite. The presence of God had sobered me up; I had never felt more clearheaded.

"Ché, you'll be okay in the morning," my best friend Jon offered. "Why don't you go and sleep it off?"

I knew sleep was not what I needed, so I told Jon and all of my friends that I was going to stop doing drugs and follow Jesus instead. Everyone in the room laughed—I probably would have been guffawing, too, if one of our other friends had found Jesus first. It seemed like an oxymoron to equate Ché with no drugs. I had been their drug supplier!

One of my friends predicted that I would get high the next day. He was wrong—it took two days. I was addicted.

There was a tug-of-war going on: I wanted to follow God, but I was addicted. I was soaring on chemicals, but deep inside I wanted to follow Christ—the Holy Spirit had already started to work in my heart. In fact, for three days I couldn't stop weeping. Off and on, the same revelation and presence of God would hit me, and I would break down and sob uncontrollably. I did not understand spiritual warfare at that time; all I knew was that there was a battle converging around me.

Making the Right Move

It took two weeks for me to fully give up drugs. It also took a dramatic encounter. My friend Jon had somehow come up with enough money to buy four tickets to see Deep Purple perform at the Baltimore Civic Center (Deep Purple was one of the hottest bands in 1973 and sang the hit song "Smoke on the Water"). Because we got the tickets at the last minute, our seats were in the back. During the performance of the warmup band, we worked our way up to the front of the auditorium to the best seats in the house. We found four spots three rows from the stage.

During the intermission, my friends walked around the auditorium, but I stayed behind to save the seats. As I sat alone, I found myself thinking about what had happened two weeks earlier when I had asked God to reveal Himself to me. I knew that Jesus was the truth, but I was having a hard time giving up drugs. In fact, both the night before and during the concert, my friends and I got high. In my pocket was a bong (pot-smoking pipe) I had smuggled in! Right there at the Deep Purple concert, I began to bargain: "God, is it okay for me to get high as long as I stay off the hard drugs and don't sell the stuff?"

It was easy for me to conclude in my own mind that since God is a God of love, He really didn't mind my smoking pot or drinking alcohol as long as I didn't hurt anyone else. I was starting to feel smug about my newfangled theology when two complete strangers sat down in my friends' seats. I leaned over to tell them that the spots were taken, but the one closest to me spoke first: "I know what you are thinking about. You think that you can do your own thing and still follow God, but you are still far from Him. You have to show Him that you are really serious about following Him."

With those words, they both got up and walked away.

To this day, I have no idea who the two strangers were. I don't know if they were angels or if they were two Christian teenagers whom God sent to me. (If they were Christians, then what they did is called prophetic evangelism, the use of gifts such as prophecy or words of knowledge to evangelize.) It really doesn't matter if they were flesh-and-blood or angelic beings, they hand-delivered a message to me.

Stunned and convicted that their words were from God, I cried out loud, "Okay, God. What do You want me to do?"

A gentle, soft voice spoke inwardly. To this day, when I close my eyes, I can still hear God's reply: "I want you to throw away your drugs and never take them again. Leave this concert and follow Me."

I took these words to mean *do it now!* From my pocket I pulled out an ounce of marijuana and some quaaludes. I also grabbed my bong. Without fanfare, I simply dropped the drugs and paraphernalia, letting the stuff crash to the floor. Then, without even waiting for my friends to return, I walked out of the civic center. That night was the last time I ever took illegal drugs. Since then, I have not even been tempted. I have been supernaturally delivered!

My friends could see the change. Word spread throughout my high school that Ché had become a Jesus freak. This was the beginning of my spiritual healing—the healing I did not know I needed. I had accepted Jesus as my Savior (see John 3:3), and then God repaired the brokenness inside me. The emptiness that I had tried to fill with drugs, sex, popularity and even Zen, He filled with joy, hope, peace, promise and so much more.

JESUS' STORY: FROM SALVATION TO HEALING

When God heals a person's body (whether ours or someone else's), quite naturally we tend to become excited. Sometimes we jump up and down and loudly praise God for what He has done. I do that! Given our human tendency toward what is sensational, this is understandable. Sometimes, however, in the wonder of the moment, we lose focus and elevate physical healing over salvation. The truth is that without salvation, the healings I have received over the years to fix my body would not be worth much. On the other hand, with salvation, such healings show me that God cares about making every part of us whole: mind, spirit and body.

Francis MacNutt puts it well:

> This is precisely how Jesus conceived his mission: the time of the Messiah would be a time of healing, of liberation, of salvation. Because the Hebrews did not think of human beings as being divided into body and soul, but as whole persons, when they spoke of salvation they thought not only of saving souls but of healing persons. And our person includes our body, our feelings, and our spirits.[1]

Virtually every person who embraces healing as a major part of his or her ministry—from Kathryn Kuhlman to Oral Roberts, from John Wimber to Benny Hinn, from myself to other local pastors—will agree on the absolute priority of salvation. Our styles and some minor theological points may differ, but for each of us, salvation is of utmost importance. Do not worry. I am not downplaying physical healing at all—

just placing everything in its proper order, which is one of the keys to seeing more healing, both spiritual and physical, occur in our midst.

YOUR STORY: FROM EMPTINESS TO WHOLENESS

I hope everyone who reads this book but doesn't yet know Jesus will pause right now and consider my story. Jesus loves you, and He came to Earth for the purpose of dying on the cross for you and for everyone else in this world. He took the punishment for all of our sins—yours and mine (see John 3:16). You may be running from God, seeking answers in all the wrong places, as I was. You may have sinned as much as I did—or more. Perhaps you hesitate to embrace the religion of your parents or to follow the beliefs of Christians in our culture. Perhaps you have been hurt by a spiritual leader, or maybe you do not understand everything about God. But because God really is who He says He is, none of these are obstacles for Him. I have been there. I have asked the questions. And I have seen God respond so wonderfully and powerfully to me and to thousands of others.

Ask Jesus to be the Lord, or boss, of your life. Surrender all that you are and all that you have to Him; and by God's grace, you will become a follower of Jesus, too. Listen for His still, small voice. He may not send you two messengers as He did for me; He may just use this book. This can be the beginning of your healing journey. True healing begins with your spirit's being healed by the Great Physician, Jesus.

To ask Jesus to be your Lord, you can pray the following prayer or one of your own. Either way, Jesus will come into your life. Go ahead and allow Him to heal your heart right now.

> *Jesus, thank You for Your love. Thank You that You died for my sins. I repent of my sins. Jesus, I believe that You died for me and rose again. Jesus, I love You and give You my life. I ask that You come into my life and take control of my life. I receive You as my Lord and Savior. From this point on, I will love You, follow You, obey You and trust You. In Jesus' name, amen.*

Note
1. Francis MacNutt, *Healing* (Notre Dame, IN: Ave Maria Press, 1999), p. 41.

Chapter 2

THE BABY-AND-THE-BATHWATER FACTOR

If I dare believe, I can be healed.

SMITH WIGGLESWORTH, *EVER INCREASING FAITH*

In my first year as a Christian I did not know much about healing. If I had a bad headache, I never thought to ask God to take it away—I just toughed it out or reached for some aspirin. If someone was very sick or hospitalized, I would pray that God would comfort him or her; and if someone was to undergo an operation, I would ask God to guide the doctors. However, I never really expected a miracle. I never dared to believe.

HEALING: IS IT FOR TODAY?

My evangelical Presbyterian leaders were good people, but they had taught me that spiritual gifts are not for today and that Jesus healed only during the New Testament period. In essence, they bypassed the New Testament instructions to pray for the sick, throwing out the proverbial baby with the bathwater.

Some Christians deemphasize or dismiss healing—and other miracles and gifts—because of a lack of understanding or an absence of experience. A few, such as my friends in my Presbyterian youth group, have a theological explanation. They subscribe to the concept that charismatic gifts (healing, prophecy, words of knowledge, etc.) have only a limited role in the life of the Church. California pastor and radio show host John MacArthur summarizes this approach: "The gift of healing, which Jesus demonstrated, was unique to Him, the 70, and the apostles."[1]

MacArthur avers what is called a dispensational, or cessationist, position. The argument goes like this: The gifts operated through Jesus and to a lesser degree through His followers in the Early Church because signs were needed to verify Jesus' messiahship. Once the Church had been fully planted, such indicators were no longer required, and thus the gifts ceased. MacArthur defines the gift of healing as the power to heal. "Jesus had it and He gave it to those who were around Him who were His representatives in order to affirm that the gospel that He was bringing and they were preaching was in fact from God," he explains.[2]

No doubt, Jesus' acts of healing were signs. The blind man could see; the lame could walk. No other rabbi had the power to change lives in such a dramatic fashion. However, two questions arise:

1. Was the gift of healing limited to Jesus and the seventy-two (some Bible versions read "the seventy") or is it still given to believers today?
2. Since Jesus healed when He walked on Earth, can He not also heal today?

I can find no Scripture that indicates that any of the gifts ended. The verse usually chosen by dispensationalists to support their claim is 1 Corinthians 13:9-10 (*NASB*): "For we know in part and we prophesy in part; but when the perfect comes, the partial will be done away." Verse 10 explains that the gifts will cease when "the perfect" comes. Some people contend that the perfect is Scripture, but verse 10 does not say "until the Word" is completed. With all due respect to MacArthur and other dispensationalists, I must contend that all of the gifts are for all believers for all time, until Jesus returns. Jesus is the perfect one, therefore the perfect will not come until He appears at the end of the age (see 1 John 3:2). In the meantime, we still need the power of the Holy Spirit to complete the task of the Great Commission and prepare for His return.

One way the Holy Spirit's power flows through us is by the gifts. When it comes to healing in particular, James does not put a time limitation on the call:

> Is any one of you sick? He should call the elders of the church to pray over him and anoint him with oil in the name of the Lord. And the prayer offered in faith will make the sick person well; the Lord will raise him up. If he has sinned, he will be forgiven (Jas. 5:14-15).

Moreover, Jesus Himself makes clear that we are to continue His works:

Truly, truly, I say to you, he who believes in Me, the works that I do, he will do also; and greater works than these he will do; because I go to the Father (John 14:12, *NASB*).

The split among Christians on the issue of healing does not revolve around whether or not Jesus has the power to heal. Most everyone agrees: He did and does. Even MacArthur, who is not at all charismatic in his doctrine and opines that miracles today are rare, allows for this: "Then we come back to the issue of does the Lord heal believers who pray for healing? And the answer to the question is, He can do whatever He wants to do."[3]

Questions, however, spring up regarding style, frequency, emphasis and the purpose of healing two thousand years after Jesus instructed the blind man to put mud in his eyes.

As I have noted, MacArthur and some other evangelicals separate the gift of healing from the act of praying for the sick, which James instructs the elders to do (see Jas. 5:14). And among respected Christian leaders who pray for the infirm and who have seen great miracles in their meetings, the terminology will vary. For example, John Wimber was known for his teaching on healing and the great miracles from God that occurred at his meetings. Yet Wimber never claimed to have the gift of healing, neither did Kathryn Kuhlman. On the other hand, Agnes Sanford and others write about people who have the gift of healing, and C. Peter Wagner lists healing among 27 gifts still active today.

I believe that the gifts have not ceased and that God does give people various gifts—both then and now. God's Word proclaims this and the evidence bears it out. In 30 years of ministry and particularly since 1994, I have seen firsthand hundreds—perhaps thousands—of people healed.

God anoints certain individuals with the gift of evangelism, the gift of teaching, the gift of prophecy, and others, including the gift of healing. This, however, does not mean that only a select few can evangelize, teach, prophesy or heal. To the contrary, the Bible makes it very clear that every believer is to do each of these.

The bottom line: We do not need the gift of healing to pray for God to heal a person. We only need to be obedient and to believe that God can and will act. An appreciation for the mystery of God doesn't hurt either!

SHARING THE GOSPEL: A NEW BOLDNESS

My senior year in high school was different from the previous years. As a Christian, I was involved in a youth group, and I caught the tail end of the Jesus movement. It actually was a very good time to be a believer.

Music has always been a big part of my life. Before knowing Jesus, I knew rock and roll. When I walked out of that Deep Purple concert, I did not have a clue about what kind of music awaited me in the Christian world. Would it be 100-year-old hymns? Gregorian chants? Southern Gospel tunes? How wonderfully surprised I was to hear Love Song, Randy Stonehill, Phil Keaggy and so many other early contemporary Christian musicians. This will date me, but I can remember when Petra released its self-titled debut album in 1974.

Our youth group put together a choir, and we sang some traditional songs and a few that were more contemporary, upbeat pieces. During spring break, a group of us went to Buffalo, New York, to visit the American side of Niagara Falls. On Palm Sunday evening, we attended a Presbyterian church.

We were the guest performers during the fellowship time after the service. During the first few selections, I sang mechanically—I was just there doing my duty. Then we started to sing "Day by Day," a song from the Broadway hit *Godspell*. The words were powerful: "To see thee more clearly / Love thee more dearly / Follow thee more nearly / Day by day." As I sang, I flung off my stuffiness and began to worship God. As I let the words sink in, I prayed, *Jesus, I really do want to see You. I want to love You with all my heart and to follow You day by day.*

> WE DO NOT NEED THE GIFT OF HEALING TO PRAY FOR GOD TO HEAL A PERSON. WE ONLY NEED TO BE OBEDIENT AND TO BELIEVE THAT GOD CAN AND WILL ACT.

As I sang, my feet began to tingle and become numb. I thought, *Oh, no, my legs have fallen asleep!* And I was standing up. The intensity of the tingling and numbness grew. Millions of zingy shots zapped through me—it felt as if I were being electrocuted. The sensation ran up my body to my head, and then down my arms to my hands. My hands were so prickly and numb that I could not close them into a fist.

This, I thought, *must be God.*

I felt His love flow all over me. I began to weep and sob. I was crying so loudly that the other young people stopped singing. My pastor, embarrassed by the overt show of emotion, dismissed me to the men's room. Still tingling all over, I wept all the way down the hall. At the time, I didn't know what was happening, but looking back, there is no question that in that moment I received God's anointing. (Some call this anointing the baptism of the Holy Spirit, or the infilling of the Holy Spirit.) I had never heard a sermon on the subject nor had I read a book about it, but my lack of theological knowledge did not stop God. He saw my open heart.

In that moment I felt what must have been just a small degree of what Jesus experienced when He said about Himself:

> The Spirit of the Lord is on me, because he has anointed me to preach good news to the poor. He has sent me to proclaim freedom for the prisoners and recovery of sight for the blind, to release the oppressed, to proclaim the year of the Lord's favor (Luke 4:18-19).

The Spirit of the Lord is likewise on me because He has anointed me to preach the good news of Jesus to the poor. God has sent me to proclaim the freedom to be found in Jesus and the recovery of sight for the blind to be found in His healing power. I likewise proclaim the year of the Lord's favor and lift Him up as the One who releases the oppressed.

How much of this did I realize that night in Buffalo? Not much at all, but after the experience, my life was never again the same. I had a new boldness to share the gospel with my friends. Up to that time, I had not led one person to Jesus. Afterward, I could not stop sharing with anyone and everyone who would listen. I was so passionately in love with Jesus that my love for Him spilled out onto others. So many people came to Christ in my high school that I started leading a prayer meeting each Wednesday morning before classes began. The gatherings continued for more than 10 years after I graduated, and this was at a public high school!

HEALING: THE FIRST TIME

Washington, D.C., in the spring is ablaze with wonderful colors and scents. Perhaps the most glorious of nature's displays are the blossoming cherry trees, imported from Japan but now a fixture along the Potomac. What an amazing exhibit of God's creative genius and what a pain for anyone, like me, who has allergies!

Despite the beauty of the season, I hated spring. As far as I was concerned, I had the worst case of allergies in the world. For three miserable months out of every year, I suffered a runny nose, itchy eyes and an asthmatic congestion that made me feel as if I were suffocating. I took medications, but nothing really worked. My father quit buying tissues because I went through too many boxes too fast. He told me to use toilet paper instead because it was cheaper. I had to bring toilet paper to school with me—talk about embarrassing!

One day, in the spring of 1974, I was wheezing away when I received a phone call from an old friend. I had known him when he was an electric guitarist in a rock band and had bought drugs from me. Rob told me that he, too, had given his life to Christ and that every Tuesday night he attended a dynamic Bible study called TAG (Take and Give—take what God gives you and give it away). He invited me to join him, so I went with him the following Tuesday. I had been a believer for one year, but it was the first time that I had attended a charismatic worship service. About 150 young people had gathered in an old gymnasium to worship God and to soak up teaching on the Word of God. They expressed their joy with abandon and passion. (The Bible study eventually grew to more than two thousand in attendance every Tuesday night.)

I walked into my first charismatic worship service with a stash of toilet paper, just in case my allergies exploded. Initially, all those people clapping and raising their hands during the vibrant worship made me feel very uncomfortable. I had grown up in a traditional church, and we never clapped, even when we wanted to applaud after a great soprano solo. However, it was not long before I began to enjoy the clapping, and I even raised my hands! As I was singing, the power of the Lord came upon me, and I was instantly healed of my allergies. My sinuses cleared, and my congestion disappeared; I could breathe again! I knew I had been supernaturally healed. It was so profound that I shouted at the top of my voice, "Praise God! I'm healed!"

Everyone stopped worshiping. The song leader stopped. The musicians stopped. Everyone stopped, and they all looked at me. I felt hundreds of eyeballs peering at me. Recovering quickly, Jim, the worship leader, said, "Praise God! This is what happens sometimes when we worship—God heals us. Let's continue to worship our great God!"

I don't remember much of the rest of that service. But I'll never forget how I felt after the service: I felt like I was floating outside, enjoying the warm spring night and breathing in the sweet air, with no allergic reactions. For the most part, I have been walking in the healing ever since. I say "for the most part" because although I have been healed of the spring allergies, I still fight an allergic reaction to certain fruits. In addition, every so often, I get an attack of sneezing, and I don't have a clue as to what causes it. Thankfully, the sneezing has never been severe enough to warrant seeing an allergist in order to determine the cause. I have simply chosen to wait on God for complete healing.

CALLING: GO FORTH
AND PRAY FOR OTHERS

When I realized that God could heal in such a dramatic way, I began to pray for anyone who wanted to be made physically whole. I volunteered as an usher at TAG. As people walked through the doors, I would greet them and ask how they were doing. Inevitably, several would share candidly that they were suffering from one ailment or another. I would ask if I could pray for them, and many received an instantaneous healing. Eventually the leaders of TAG approached me, saying, "It is obvious that God has given you the gift of healing. Why don't you pray about being one of our prayer counselors?" They were referring to 1 Corinthians 12:9, which speaks of the gifts of healing that the Holy Spirit gives.

I was honored.

Within a year, the leaders asked me to oversee the healing room. And so, from 1975 through the end of 1979, when TAG ended, I prayed for the sick every Tuesday night. There, God began to teach me the principles of healing—principles that I am still learning today. It is my hope that as I share these principles with you, they will help you receive your own healing. More important, I pray that you will be equipped to minister to others.

Father, I pray that this book will be used to heal many. I pray that people reading this book will receive a greater revelation of Your extravagant love for them and how it is Your will for them to be healed. I also ask that this book will equip Your Church to move in the healing anointing. I pray for a supernatural impartation to heal the sick so that we can compassionately reach a lost and suffering world. In Jesus' name, amen.

Notes

1. John MacArthur, Jr., *Bible Questions and Answers* (Panorama City, CA: Word of Grace, 2000), audiocassette no. GC 70-19, quoted at *Bible Bulletin Board*.   http://www.biblebb.com/files/macqa/70-19-8.htm (accessed August 29, 2003).

2. Ibid.

3. Ibid.

Chapter 3

THE AUTHORITY
FACTOR

The kingdom of God is demonstrated by releasing the spiritual
authority necessary for performing signs, wonders and miracles.
BARBARA WENTROBLE, *PRAYING WITH AUTHORITY*

In 2000, I was busy preparing for The Call DC, a massive
prayer gathering of young people in our nation's capital.[1] Prior
to the solemn assembly, I traveled to cities on the East Coast
to spread the word and encourage people to join us. One of my
stops was Philadelphia. It was there that I met John and
Sharon Trainor. And it was there that God exhibited an
incredible bodily healing.

Jack and Jane Hanley, members of Harvest International

Ministries (an apostolic network of pastors and people in ministry and an extension of my ministry), had organized a get-together in Philadelphia and asked me to speak. The emphasis that Monday night was on healing. One of the women in attendance that night was Sharon Trainor, a new believer, accompanied by her husband, John, who was not a believer.

Doctors had diagnosed Sharon with an incurable problem called reflex sympathetic dystrophy syndrome (RSDS). For more than eight years she had suffered excruciating pain in her feet. Two surgeries to cut the nerves to her feet in an effort to eliminate the pain did not work, nor did the steroids and painkillers. Her pain was so great that even a bedsheet touching her feet caused overwhelming pain.

Sharon was confined mostly to a wheelchair but occasionally could walk with a walker or with the assistance of another person. She and John had come to the service because they were desperate for her to be healed. It was worth giving God a shot at reversing a condition that had stumped even the best medical professionals.

At the meeting, I gave the invitation for people to give their hearts and lives to Jesus. Sharon renewed her commitment to the Lord, and John said yes right along with her. I followed the altar call with a prayer for people to be healed and spoke a few words of knowledge. People were healed but not Sharon. I announced that I would stick around after the meeting and personally pray for those who hadn't receive a manifestation of God's touch.

Many people lined up for prayer. When I came to John and Sharon, I didn't have time to ask them about her condition, but it was obvious that something was wrong with her feet—she was wearing oversized, pink terrycloth bathroom slippers. Just as I noticed the slippers, the authority of God came over me. I broke every generational curse (I write more about this in chapter 7) and commanded the evil spirits to leave her. As soon as I took authority, both John and Sharon fell backward. Sharon had had her eyes closed, so she asked her husband if I had pushed her down.

John was very protective of his wife and didn't trust faith healers, so he had had his eyes wide open. He told her that I hadn't touched either of them. It only took one more moment for Sharon to realize that her feet felt normal. After so many years of agony, there was no more pain. It was gone!

> ## ALL PHYSICAL MALADIES, INCLUDING THE ULTIMATE—BODILY DEATH—CAME ABOUT ONLY AFTER THE DOOR TO SIN SWUNG OPEN.

The situation grew a bit comical as John and Sharon refused to move or get off the floor; they were afraid that they would jinx the healing. Finally, Jack Hanley had to ask them to leave because he was closing up the building—they were the last ones out.

That night, as John and Sharon drove away from the church, they didn't say one word to each other, still afraid the healing would disappear. When they got home, Sharon immediately went to bed and fell asleep. The next morning, she was certain that her whole experience had been a dream—but she didn't feel any pain. So she tested her feet. Getting out of bed, she placed them on the floor—still no pain! That is when she knew she had been healed.

Sharon started to dance and run through the house. She tracked down Jack's telephone number and told him the story.

By this time I was in Harrisburg, Pennsylvania, but Jack told me what had happened. To say the least, we all rejoiced at this miraculous healing.

A Fallen World

What is divine healing? Scholar Ronald A. N. Kydd calls it "restoration of health through the direct intervention of God. The products of such intervention are miracles. This kind of healing is divine because of God's involvement. It occurs because God acts."[2]

God acts because we need Him to act, but He never intended for there to be healing. Why? He never set out to mend hearts, because He never wanted them broken. He never aimed to miraculously reverse cancer, because malignant tumors were not part of His original plan. God's aspirations for Adam and Eve did not call for healing, because His plan did not include sickness. There was no need for aspirin, flu shots or HMOs in the Garden of Eden. That all changed with the Fall. When Adam and Eve listened to the serpent and ate the fruit that God had commanded them not to eat, sin entered the world. With sin came separation from God and His perfect plans. All physical maladies, including the ultimate—bodily death—came about only after this door to sin swung open.

Jews for Jesus founder Moishe Rosen put it well in the title of one of his books—*The Universe Is Broken: Who on Earth Can Fix It?* In other words, all of God's creation, including our human bodies, is infected by sin. In fact, as we go along in life, we are naturally prone to disease, destruction and all kinds of hurt and pain. How did it end up this way, and who can fix it?

Before the Fall

From the beginning, God planned for man and woman to rule and reign with Him. He gave Adam and Eve tremendous authority in order to do this. In Genesis 1:27-28, the Bible states:

> So God created man in his own image, in the image of God he created him; male and female he created them. God blessed them and said to them, "Be fruitful and increase in number; fill the earth and *subdue* it. *Rule* over the fish of the sea and the birds of the air and over every living creature that moves on the ground" (emphasis added).

The Hebrew word used for "subdue" in this context is *kabash,* which means to conquer hostile forces (see Num. 32:22,29; Josh. 18:1, *NASB*). Gregory Boyd wrote the book *God at War,* in which he expressed his belief that from the beginning of humankind's creation, there were demonic forces on Earth and that we were meant to have dominion over them.

According to God's hierarchy, as described in the Bible, it is clear that next to God, we have the highest authority. In Psalm 8:5, David wrote, "You made him [humankind] a little lower than the heavenly beings and crowned him with glory and honor." The word used here for "heavenly beings" is *elohim,* which can also be translated as "God." God made us a little lower than Him! Unfortunately, when Adam and Eve chose to sin, they lost their God-given authority, and Satan claimed authority on Earth from humankind.

Satan's Position

The Bible makes it clear that Satan possesses authority:

> Again, the devil took him to a very high mountain and showed him all the kingdoms of the world and their splendor. "All this I will give you," he said, "if you will bow down and worship me." Jesus said to him, "Away from me, Satan! For it is written: 'Worship the Lord your God, and serve him only'" (Matt. 4:8-10).

Satan couldn't have offered Jesus the kingdoms of the world if he didn't have the authority to do so. Satan became the ruler of this world after the Fall.

John 14:30 quotes Jesus: "I will no longer talk much with you, for the *ruler of this world* is coming, and he has nothing in Me" (*NKJV*, emphasis added). Jesus clearly acknowledged that at that point Satan was the ruler of the world.

Jesus' Victory

Jesus had a plan to destroy the works of the devil and take away Satan's authority. First John 3:8 reads, "He who does what is sinful is of the devil, because the devil has been sinning from the beginning." The Son of God came to Earth in order to destroy the devil's work and reconcile humankind to the Father.

John 12:31-33 quotes Jesus: "Now is the time for judgment on this world; now the prince of this world will be driven out. But I, when I am lifted up from the earth, will draw all men to myself." Jesus would drive out the enemy by stripping him of his authority, thus leading to the salvation of many. How did He do this?

When Jesus went to the cross, He was pure and without sin. Satan had nothing on Him. While on the cross, Jesus took the authority back from the devil. There are a number of verses to support this:

1. Colossians 2:14-15—"Having canceled the written code, with its regulations, that was against us and that stood opposed to us; he took it away, nailing it to the cross. *And having disarmed the powers and authorities*, he made a public spectacle of them, triumphing over them *by the cross*" (emphasis added).

2. First Corinthians 2:8—"None of the rulers of this age understood it, for if they had, they would not have crucified the Lord of glory." This is an amazing verse! Essentially, the Bible is saying that if Satan and his cohorts had known they would be stripped of their authority, they never would have crucified Jesus! I don't fully understand what happened on the cross, but I know that Jesus not only took our place on it and became sin on our behalf (see 2 Cor. 5:21), but he also took authority back from Satan.

3. Matthew 28:18-20—"*All authority in heaven and on earth has been given to me.* Therefore go and make disciples of all nations, baptizing them in the name of the Father and of the Son and of the Holy Spirit, and teaching them to obey everything I have commanded you. And surely I am with you always, to the very end of the age" (emphasis added). These words of Jesus provide conclusive evidence.

Our Position in Christ

Not only has Jesus taken authority from the enemy, but He has also placed His followers in a position of authority with Him. In Ephesians 1:17-23, Paul wrote:

> I keep asking that the God of our Lord Jesus Christ, the glorious Father, may give you the Spirit of wisdom and revelation, so that you may know him better. I pray also that the eyes of your heart may be enlightened in order that you may know the hope to which he has called you, the riches of his glorious inheritance in the saints, and his incomparably great power for us who believe. That power is like the working of his mighty strength, which he exerted in Christ when he raised him from the dead and seated him at his right hand in the heavenly realms, far above all rule and authority, power and dominion, and every title that can be given, not only in the present age but also in the one to come. And God placed all things under his feet and appointed him to be head over everything for the church, which is his body, the fullness of him who fills everything in every way.

God states clearly that we, as believers, are seated with Christ in the heavenly places: "And God raised us up with Christ and seated us with him in the heavenly realms in Christ Jesus" (Eph. 2:6). If God has placed all rule and authority under His feet and if we, the Church, are His Body, then we have a part in Christ's authority over all power and dominion as well.

Revelation 5:10 makes it clear that we are to reign with Christ on Earth: "And [You, Jesus] have made us kings and priests to our God; and we shall reign on the earth" (*NKJV*). This leads to the truth about our authority in Christ.

OUR AUTHORITY IN CHRIST

In November of 1998, I had a divine revelation regarding our authority in Christ. I recount it in my book *The Authority of the Believer and Healing*.[3] I want to focus in this book on the scriptural foundation concerning our authority in Christ because of another divine encounter I had.

In January of 2001, John and Carol Arnott came to Harvest Rock Church to minister over a weekend. It is hard for me to explain exactly what happened, but during one service, Carol started to pray for me. When she did, I fell to the floor. For more than an hour I felt like I was in a boxing match with Satan. I also heard the Lord speak to me repeatedly: "My people are destroyed from lack of knowledge" (Hos. 4:6). The Lord was saying to me: "God's people are being destroyed by the ignorance of their authority in Christ."

Righteous anger arose within me during that time. I saw how the Church had been suffering unnecessary casualties of supernatural war by not engaging in battle with the authority that Jesus had given. After I heard this message, I made a decision to try my best to educate believers on the authority that Christ has given us. This chapter is, in part, a result of that decision.

The way I read the Gospel of Matthew, Peter and the Church have authority over spirits.

> And I tell you that you are Peter, and on this rock I will build my church, and the gates of Hades will not overcome it. I will give you the keys of the kingdom of

heaven; whatever you bind on earth will be bound in heaven, and whatever you loose on earth will be loosed in heaven (16:18-19).

Luke 10:18-19 adds to the case:

[Jesus] replied, "I saw Satan fall like lightning from heaven. I have given you authority to trample on snakes and scorpions and to overcome all the power of the enemy; nothing will harm you."

The apostle John wrote in Revelation 12:10-11:

Then I heard a loud voice in heaven say: "Now have come the salvation and the power and the kingdom of our God, and the authority of his Christ. For the accuser of our brothers, who accuses them before our God day and night, has been hurled down. *They overcame him* by the blood of the Lamb and by the word of their testimony; they did not love their lives so much as to shrink from death" (emphasis added).

As I shared in my book *The Authority of the Believer and Healing,* the authority God has given to believers is the key to fulfilling the Great Commission (see Matt. 28:18-20).[4] We have the authority to expand His kingdom by healing the sick and casting out demons (see Mark 16:15-18).

He called his twelve disciples to him and gave them authority to drive out evil spirits and to heal every disease and sickness (Matt. 10:1).

When Jesus had called the Twelve together, he gave them power and authority to drive out all demons and to cure diseases, and he sent them out to preach the kingdom of God and to heal the sick (Luke 9:1-2).

It is my conviction that as we grow in authority, we will see greater miracles and more healings than we do now.

> WE HAVE THE AUTHORITY
> TO EXPAND GOD'S KINGDOM
> BY HEALING THE SICK AND
> CASTING OUT DEMONS.

REMOVE THE HINDRANCES

Let me close by sharing several reasons why the Church does not exercise her authority in Christ.

Sin

1. When we habitually sin, we come under Satan's authority, and he has legal rights over us until we repent. That is why Jesus said, "The prince of the world has nothing on me" (see John 14:30). Jesus was without sin and the devil could not get a foothold in His life.

2. Ephesians 2:1-2 (*NKJV*) expresses, "And you He made alive, who were dead in trespasses and sins, in which you once walked according to the course of

this world, according to the prince of the power of the air, the spirit who now works in the sons of disobedience."

3. Colossians 1:13-14 states, "For he has rescued us from the dominion of darkness and brought us into the kingdom of the Son he loves, in whom we have redemption, the forgiveness of sins."

4. First John 5:18-19 says, "We know that anyone born of God does not continue to sin; the one who was born of God keeps him safe, and the evil one cannot harm him. We know that we are children of God, and that the whole world is under the control of the evil one."

5. James 5:16 declares, "The prayer of a righteous man is powerful and effective."

Authority is given to the righteous. Carlos Annacondia, an Argentine evangelist, once told me that he believes that God gave him more authority when he became ruthless about his sin and the sin in his family's life. Along the same line, we have to be under authority before we can exercise authority. If we are rebellious toward our parents or the authority of our church, we won't have much authority over the evil one.

Ignorance

1. In Hosea 4:6, God declares, "My people are destroyed from lack of knowledge."

2. Second Corinthians 10:3-5 states, "For though we live in the world, we do not wage war as the world does. The weapons we fight with are not the weapons of the world. On the contrary, they have divine power to demolish strongholds. We demolish

arguments and every pretension that sets itself up against the knowledge of God, and we take captive every thought to make it obedient to Christ."

Many believers tend to see the cosmic struggle through the lens of the Asian philosophy of yin and yang, which contends that good and evil forces are opposite each other but equal in power and authority. In reality, Satan is a sure loser. Satan is a created being, one of God's fallen angels. God is the uncreated Creator who always has been and always will be—He is self-existent. To a believer who is walking in God's authority, Satan is like a toothless lion. It is not that Satan doesn't have some real power—he does. But when we compare his power with God's—there is *no comparison*.

When David confronted Goliath, Goliath compared his physical prowess with David's. Goliath was insulted that the Israelites would send a mere shepherd boy against him. However, David didn't compare himself with Goliath; he compared Goliath with God. God was so much greater than Goliath that the match was over before it had a chance to begin (see 1 Sam. 17:41-50).

As I have observed God's people, I have noticed that way too many of us tend to be ignorant about the source of evil. Satan, not God, is the cause of all the evil in the world.[5] When we have a warped perspective of the sovereignty of God, we become passive in fighting sickness and evil. After the historic tragedy of 9/11 in New York, I was amazed how many people attributed the attacks to God's judgment. The Bible tells me that Satan is the one who comes to kill, steal and destroy (see John 10:10), and that we are to put on the full armor of God and to stand firm against the evil one (see Eph. 6:10-18).

Unbelief

Unbelief is a serious sin. Romans 14:23 reads, "But the man who has doubts is condemned if he eats, because his eating is not from faith; and everything that does not come from faith is sin." The book of Hebrews calls unbelief sinful: "See to it, brothers, that none of you has a sinful, unbelieving heart that turns away from the living God" (3:12). Unbelief is so serious that Jesus could not do many miracles because of the people's unbelief (see Matt. 13:58).

We can measure the level of our belief or unbelief by asking ourselves, *Do we really believe that Jesus defeated the enemy?*

Fear

1. Second Timothy 1:7-8 (*NKJV*) declares, "God has not given us a spirit of fear."

2. First John 5:18 teaches us that "the evil one cannot harm [anyone born of God]" (see also Luke 10:19). But some people have suffered backlash from the enemy when engaged in spiritual warfare and are now afraid. There are many reasons for backlash. Here are some ways to guard against it: Be led by the Spirit; make sure that Satan has no legal rights to attack; and obtain prayer covering. After covering these bases, we *can* confront the darkness, because we *have* authority to do so. We can conduct strategic warfare because we have authority, and we must obey God's directives.[6]

3. Luke 12:32 gives us wise counsel: "Do not be afraid, little flock, for your Father has been pleased to give you the kingdom."

Prayerlessness

1. Luke 18:1 establishes the importance of prayer: "Then Jesus told his disciples a parable to show them that they should always pray and not give up."

2. Ephesians 6:18 elaborates on this point: "And pray in the Spirit on all occasions with all kinds of prayers and requests. With this in mind, be alert and always keep on praying for all the saints."

Evangelist Winkie Pratney once told a story about a pastor's wife who was jogging one day when she saw a man dressed in white standing in a cornfield. The pastor's wife had been going through a difficult trial, and when she saw this man, whom she recognized as Jesus, He said to her, "Don't you know who I am? Don't you know who you are? When you know this, it is not really as hard as you think." There is a lesson here for all of us. When we know who God is and the authority He has, and when we know who we are in Christ, having faith is not that difficult.[7]

Dear God, I repent of and renounce all fear, unbelief and bad theology. Today let me start exercising the authority You have given me. Thank You. Amen.

Notes

1. The Call's purpose is to shape history by gathering all generations to massive prayer, fasting and humble repentance. Over 400,000 young people attended this historic gathering in Washington, D.C. For more information on The Call, check out the website www.thecall.com.
2. Ronald A. N. Kydd, *Healing Through the Centuries: Models for Understanding* (Peabody, MA: Hendrickson Publishers, 2001), p. xv.
3. Ché Ahn, *The Authority of the Believer and Healing* (Colorado Springs, CO: Wagner Publications, 1999), pp. 36-37.
4. Ibid., p. 19.
5. The literary phrase "I am going to bring disaster on [certain people or groups]," which occurs quite a few times in Scripture (see 1 Kings 14:10; 2 Chron. 34:24,28; Jer. 4:6; 6:19; Ezek. 5:17), is actually describing the consequences of sin.
6. For more information about this spiritual battle and how believers can be victorious, read Cindy Jacobs, *Possessing the Gates of the Enemy* (Shippensburg, PA: Destiny Image, 1994) and Chuck D. Pierce, *The Worship Warrior* (Ventura, CA: Regal Books, 2002).
7. Winkie Pratney, speaking at Harvest Rock Church, n.d.

Chapter 4

THE POWER FACTOR

What is the anointing? It is the power of God.
BENNY HINN, *THE ANOINTING*

The man was disheveled and claimed to be homeless. He had heard the music and had come into the tent set up on Hollywood Boulevard to see what was happening inside. He sat and listened as Benny Hinn preached, leaning to the right so he could hear with his one good ear. Benny was in classic form, telling stories of times when God had moved at similar meetings and teaching about how to deepen one's faith.

Several hundred people sat on folding chairs and hung on Hinn's every word. Christians in the crowd knew what was coming next. After the Word had been preached, the Israeli-born evangelist of Armenian descent began to call out various physical maladies: "Someone here has diabetes." "There is a woman with cancer." "A man cannot hear out of his left ear."

At that last comment, the disheveled man nearly leaped to his feet. When Hinn called forward those with the ailments he had called out, the man was nearly first in line.

"God wants to heal you tonight," Hinn said, placing his hand on each person who stood before him on the platform. Most fell over backward into the arms of men who had been placed there to act as catchers. These men gently lowered to the floor those who had fallen backward. There, a man with diabetes, a woman with cancer and the homeless man with only one good ear lay prostrate. In Pentecostal and charismatic circles, this has become known as being slain in the Spirit. It is in this position that God often reaches into the deepest crevices of people's souls and often heals their bodies—especially under the ministries of people who, like Hinn, flow in the anointing. I have seen this happen often at my church, Harvest Rock Church, in Pasadena, California, and when I'm speaking on the road.

What is this anointing? From where does this power come? Does it have to come through the hands of the anointed such as Hinn? Do we have to fall over backward to receive the healing?

Was the man who claimed to be homeless healed?

Jumping up and down as if he were plugged in to a power outlet, the man told Hinn that his left ear had popped open. "It felt like electricity," he said. "I can hear!" Hinn cupped his hand over the man's right ear. "I can hear!" the disheveled man declared.[1]

Benny Hinn flows in what I call an individual anointing. God uses men and women such as Hinn and Kathryn Kuhlman as conduits for healing. His power flows through them so that others may be whole. Yet in God's wonderful and mysterious modes, that is by no means the only way the anointing flows.

When we need to be healed or know someone who does, we want to go to where the power is. Of course, the Holy Spirit is the only source, but God uses a variety of modes to get that healing power to our bodies. In addition to its flowing from an individual, healing can also happen with no human touch at all.

HOW THE POWER FLOWS

We do not want to make this a formula—God will surprise us by working in a new way as soon as we do that. However, there are certain modes God has established in the Bible and by which He also moves today. Here we look at both individual anointing and corporate power.

Individual Anointing

To move in the healing anointing, we need the power of the Holy Spirit. Jesus received that power when John the Baptist baptized Him in the Jordan River (see Luke 3:21-22). From that point on, Jesus began to heal the sick and cast out demons by the power of the Spirit. Following His baptism, Christ referred to Isaiah 61:

> The Spirit of the Lord is on me, because he has anointed me to preach good news to the poor. He has sent me to proclaim freedom for the prisoners and recovery of sight for the blind, to release the oppressed, to proclaim the year of the Lord's favor (Luke 4:18-19).

Jesus had real, tangible power. When the woman with the

issue of blood came up to Him and touched the hem of His garment, she was instantly healed (see Mark 5:25-30). The Bible reports, "At once Jesus realized that power had gone out from him" (v. 30).

The disciples also had this power at work in their ministry. In fact, the Holy Spirit's capacity to heal is so powerful that it was transferred even through items of clothing: "God did extraordinary miracles through Paul, so that even handkerchiefs and aprons that had touched him were taken to the sick, and their illnesses were cured and the evil spirits left them" (Acts 19:11-12).

When Peter's shadow fell on the sick, they were healed (see Acts 5:15)—it was not his shadow specifically that worked the miracle; rather, it was the power of the Lord radiating from him, producing signs and wonders.

This all may sound odd to us in the new millennium, but these events are declared in the Bible, and besides, God can do whatever He wants. Even today such healings occur. Many people have rolled their eyes when Oral Roberts and others have sent out anointed prayer cloths and have questioned if the cloths could possibly work. Indeed, the Oral Roberts Evangelistic Association and other ministries are replete with contemporary testimonies of people who claim they have been healed after receiving an anointed item.

Benny Hinn explains this dynamic well:

The presence of God the Holy Spirit leads to the anointing of the Spirit, which is the power of God, and the power of God brings forth the manifestation of the presence. The anointing itself—an anointing of the Holy Spirit—cannot be seen, but the power, its manifestations, its effects, can and should be seen.[2]

I, too, have witnessed this manifestation of powerful healing.

A Thanksgiving Miracle

Every year at Thanksgiving, we host a brief one-hour service at Harvest Rock Church. We want to give thanks to the Lord for what He has done during the year. Before the event, we tell our members, "As you're going 'over the river and through the woods to Grandmother's house,' make a pit stop at our Thanksgiving Day service." We also encourage them to invite unbelievers.

While we generally design our Sunday services for the believer, our Thanksgiving service is very seeker sensitive—it is prime time to bring relatives and friends who would not regularly come to church. The worship is brief, and we have people give testimonies of what God has done in their lives. I (or another staff member) usually give a short message and invite people to accept Christ as their Savior.

Such was the setting on Thanksgiving 1998. I was glad to express thanks at church, but I also was eager for the traditional meal that would follow at my home. I was not particularly looking for miracles that day and had no advanced warning as to what would happen.

A church member named Harriet came to the service that day and brought with her a woman from Sri Lanka. The visitor did not come forward to receive Christ when the invitation was given, but she and Harriet approached me afterward to ask for prayer. When Harriet introduced me to her friend, she leaned over to me and whispered that the Sri Lankan woman was not a Christian.

"So what can I do for you?" I asked the woman.

"Please pray for me that I may have a baby," she replied. "My husband and I have been married for seven years, and we have spent thousands of dollars for fertility treatments, but I cannot have a baby. I even went to India recently to have a special treatment, but nothing has worked. And now my husband is ready to leave me because I cannot give him a child."

The woman was desperate and in obvious distress.

I never turn down a request for prayer and am always eager to see how God will answer. Given that, I started to intercede. To be honest, it was a typical prayer. I asked God to allow the woman to conceive and have a baby. As I was about to say amen, I felt the Holy Spirit come over me, and to my astonishment, I prophesied, "You will have a child within one year!"

The instant I said those words, two things happened. The woman collapsed onto the floor under the power of the Holy Spirit, even though I hadn't touched her. The prophetic word released a tangible power that knocked her to the floor. In addition, I immediately wanted to take back the prophecy— not the part about having a baby; I had faith for that. But I wanted to retract the specific time frame: I had declared that she would have a baby *within one year!* As a rule of thumb, I teach that when we prophesy, we should not give specific dates. The word may be true, but if the specific date is off, then the prophecy will be discredited. This time it was too late. I had set a date, and she was lying on the floor—there hadn't even been a catcher (but she was not hurt). Since I could not retract what I had said, I decided to once more be a fool for Christ and trust God.

I didn't see the woman from Sri Lanka the following Sunday, and frankly, I forgot about her until a month later. At the Christmas service she approached me. With her were Harriet and a man I presumed to be her husband.

"Do you remember me?" she beamed, her face almost aglow.

I hate it when people ask me that. Youth With A Mission founder Loren Cunningham has a gift for remembering the name of virtually everyone he meets—that's great for him. However, I must confess, I do not. I see so many people during my travels, and we have quite a few visitors at Harvest Rock Church, so I almost invariably don't remember them.

"No, please forgive me. I don't remember," I replied.

"You prayed for me last month to get pregnant," she recounted.

It came back to me. "Yes, I remember now."

"I am happy to tell you that I am three weeks pregnant!"

As a result of her miraculous pregnancy—a tangible manifestation of not only God's power but His love as well—this woman and her husband gave their lives to Jesus that Sunday. Nine months later, we (the parents and I) had the privilege of dedicating to the Lord a beautiful baby girl during a Sunday morning service. Hallelujah!

Corporate Power

Another dimension of God's power can produce healing. I call it corporate power: the tangible power of the Holy Spirit, manifested in the atmosphere of a given room or place. Some people call it the glory of God, or the manifest presence of God. I simply call it corporate power based on Luke 5:17. This passage recounts the time Jesus was in Peter's home in Capernaum "and the power of the Lord was present for him to heal the sick." We know that Jesus already had power, but in this instance we see that the power was also *present* in the room.

We see corporate anointing even at meetings of individuals who are anointed to heal. Many people who attended services conducted by Kathryn Kuhlman recount how the power in the auditorium was so tangible that people would be healed just sitting in their seats, sometimes waiting for the service to begin. This is also true in the healing services of Benny Hinn. I have seen people healed without anyone's praying for them or any word of knowledge being directed toward them. The manifestation of God's tangible power comes and heals them supernaturally.

How exactly does this happen? Ah, again we see the mystery of God at work. My personal experience with spring allergies is an example of healing by this corporate power of God (see chapter 2). I shared another example in my first book, *Into the Fire*. A young girl named Jenny was instantly healed of partial deafness at a Sunday worship service. At first, she thought that her hearing aid was malfunctioning, because the sound was so loud. She took out her hearing aid and realized that without it she could hear perfectly for the first time in her life. No one had prayed for her. She was not at a special healing service. She received her healing sovereignly on a typical Sunday morning that became anything but typical for her.

People with myriad illnesses throng to services of the better-known evangelists who have healing ministries. God, however, is not limited to working at Kathryn Kuhlman or Benny Hinn meetings, nor is He restricted to working at Harvest Rock Church or in other congregations such as ours.

Testimonies come from around the globe. Evangelist Reinhard Bonnke tells of healings in Africa. San Jose, California, pastor Dick Bernal recounts how God miraculously touched people in a crowd in India. *700 Club* host Pat Robertson tells of one time when a person who was not even watching the show was healed: A friend had called in the request for prayer, and at the moment of the prayer, God acted.

A Miracle in Mexico

Healing does not have to be dramatic. Sometimes it can be verified by a doctor; at other times it is something solely between God and the person who has been restored to health. Nonetheless, it does catch our attention when our God, the Great Physician, acts in a mighty and visible way.

By far, the most dramatic example I can give is a healing that took place in Juarez, Mexico. In April 1997, I was asked to conduct a pastors' conference in the Mexican metropolis, which is just across the border from El Paso, Texas. I was to speak at a wonderful church pastored by Victor Richards.

At the end of a teaching session, people lined up around the periphery of the large building to give testimony of how God had touched them during the meeting. Suddenly, I noticed a commotion in the rear of the auditorium. I asked

> WE WILL SEE MORE SOVEREIGN HEALINGS AS WE LEARN HOW TO HOST THE HOLY SPIRIT NOT ONLY IN OUR SUNDAY MORNING SERVICES BUT IN OUR HOMES AND LIVES AS WELL.

Carlos Quintero, a friend and Los Angeles pastor who had come with me to Juarez, to investigate. A few minutes later, he returned to the platform with a middle-aged Mexican woman at his side. "We've got to let her testify!" he exclaimed.

The testimony that unfolded in the next few minutes was nothing short of incredible. A hydrocephalic woman, whom the doctors had declared to have only two months to live and who had been unable to walk or talk, had been completely healed of her infirmity! (Hydrocephalus is also known as water on the brain.) As she recounted what happened, the audience exploded in a roar of praise and thanksgiving. What a demonstration of God's power!

PLUG IN TO THE SOURCE

It would take me days and days to recount all of the times that I have seen evidence of the tangible power of God. Indeed, God still heals in our times. Thank God for Benny Hinn and others like him. God is moving in the services in which they minister. However, we are not all Benny Hinns, and God does move in so many other places. I believe that we will see more such sovereign healings as we learn how to host the Holy Spirit not only in our Sunday morning services but in our homes and lives as well.

Where are we to begin if we need a healing or if we want to pray for a healing? Here are four action steps that will help anyone make a good beginning:

1. Be full of the Holy Spirit. Receive the power of the Holy Spirit.[3]
2. Go to a healing service where the Holy Spirit is known to be moving.
3. Invite the Holy Spirit to come to your house. Learn how to host the Holy Spirit.[4]
4. Receive prayer from someone who has the gift of healing or an anointing to heal. Allow the tangible power of God to touch you through one of His anointed servants.

Perhaps part of the reason God shrouds His anointing in

mystery is so that it will be fresh, that we will not turn to it as a ritual or proceed in it by rote. Toronto pastor John Arnott saw great moves of the Spirit during meetings at his church in what has become known as the Toronto Blessing. Arnott warns: "Unless we treasure God's presence when He comes and make it a point to keep watch over our hearts, we can become so accustomed to the anointing that we begin to treat the Spirit like part of the furnishings and décor."[5]

Dear God, I want to walk in the fullness of Your Spirit. Please fill me now. Let Your power flow to me and through me. Show me how to host Your Holy Spirit in my life, my home, my church and my relationships with others. Thank You for Your anointed servants. Let Your healing power flow through those whom You have gifted for healing. And let people who are touched by Your corporate power be healed everywhere. Amen.

Notes

1. Reported by Steven Lawson, who attended Sonset Ministries' "Rejoice Hollywood" outreach where Benny Hinn spoke in April 2003.
2. Benny Hinn, *The Anointing* (Nashville, TN: Thomas Nelson Publishers, 1992), p. 74.
3. For more information on the power of the Holy Spirit, read C. Peter Wagner, *Acts of the Holy Spirit* (Ventura, CA: Regal Books, 1994). For specific information about the baptism of the Holy Spirit, see C. Peter Wagner, *Acts of the Holy Spirit*, pp. 54-55.
4. For more teaching on how to host the Holy Spirit, read Ché Ahn, *Hosting the Holy Spirit* (Ventura, CA: Renew Books, 2000).
5. John Arnott, "Valuing the Anointing," in Ché Ahn, ed., *Hosting the Holy Spirit* (Ventura, CA: Renew Books, 2000), p. 10.

Chapter 5

THE FAITH FACTOR

Faith means having chutzpah.
FRANCIS MACNUTT, *HEALING*

*Christ promised the signs, and they followed as long as Christians
continued to believe and expect them.*
A. B. SIMPSON, *THE GOSPEL OF HEALING*

When we pray for healing, we need faith. When we need to be healed, we need faith. To have faith means to believe God and to act upon that belief. Abraham was a great model for us when it comes to faith.

And the scripture was fulfilled that says, "Abraham believed God, and it was credited to him as righteousness," and he was called God's friend (Jas. 2:23).

FRIENDS OF GOD

More than anything else, I long to be a friend of God. Intellectually, I know we are all friends of God. Jesus made this ultimately clear when He said, "No longer do I call you servants but friends" (see John 15:15). However, friendship is just the starting point of a relationship. I believe there is a level of intimacy of love and friendship that Jesus wants to have with each one of us, beginning with and building on the relationship provided by the finished work of the Cross. That is why we are called not only friends of God but also the Bride of Christ (see Rev. 19:7).

Abraham had that kind of close friendship with God. What amazes me is that Abraham was in many ways a scoundrel. Twice he pimped his wife, Sarah, in order to save his own selfish neck. He got impatient for the child God promised him, so at Sarah's urging, he had sex with Hagar. Ishmael was born as a result, and to this day, the Arabs, Ishmael's descendants, have been a thorn in the flesh of Israel. Yet God called Abraham "friend." Why? Because Abraham had extraordinary faith: "Abraham believed God."

Abraham's faith was so strong that even when God told him to sacrifice his son Isaac, he still believed that someday he would have as many descendants as the stars in heaven and the grains of sand on the ground, as God had promised. This is why in Genesis 22:5 Abraham told his servants, "Stay here with the donkey while I and the boy go over there. We will worship and then we will come back to you." Abraham believed that he and Isaac would return. The writer of Hebrews hints that

Abraham thought God would raise Isaac from the dead after he had sacrificed him. Of course, this proved to be unnecessary, since Abraham passed the test of faith (see Gen. 22:15-17; Heb. 11:19).

The Bible makes it clear that it is impossible to please God without faith (see Heb. 11:6). God honors those who believe in Him (see Heb. 12). This is why His heroes are usually simple people instead of the rich, the powerful or the famous. The simple act of true faith is a crucial principle of healing. Over and over again we see people who were healed because of, and subsequently commended for, their faith. Conversely, we see that Jesus withheld miracles because of the unbelief of the people.

A DEEP SUBJECT

Faith is such a vital component in our lives if we truly want to live for God. It is a complex subject, so there is no way to do it justice in one chapter. Entire books have been written on the subject of faith. In fact, Chuck Pierce and Robert Heidler have penned *Restoring Your Shield of Faith*, which delves deep into the ways faith can be applied today, especially in spiritual warfare.[1]

When we talk about faith, we often use it as a general term to describe every aspect of our relationship with God. Faith, obviously, is more specific than that as well. Faith is the very fiber of the connection between God and us. It is the essential element that enables us to go forward as servants and look back in praise. Without faith we could not be faithful. It means we put our whole trust in God. It means we trust our entire present and future to Him. It has been said that when we follow Jesus in faith, we are to keep our eyes locked on Him and follow His every step. Along the way of life there will be trees with branches that hang low. If we constantly shift our focus between Jesus and the branches, then we are likely to lose our step, stumble and fall. If we keep our eyes on Jesus and duck when He ducks, we will miss all of the branches—in fact, we will never have even seen most of them.

When it comes to healing, faith plays an integral part.

> # WHEN IT COMES TO HEALING, FAITH PLAYS AN INTEGRAL PART.

AGENTS OF HEALING

C. Peter Wagner identifies three agents of faith connected with healing.

> The New Testament has examples of three different possible agents of the faith necessary for divine healing to take place, the sick person being only one of the possible agents. . . .
>
> Another agent is an intermediary. A Roman centurion once asked Jesus for healing on behalf of his servant who was paralyzed, perhaps much like the lame man at the Temple gate. In this case, Jesus congratulated the centurion and said, "I have not found such great *faith*, not even in Israel!" (Matt. 8:10, italics

added). Not only did the ailing servant have no faith, but he probably had no idea even who Jesus was or that his master was asking for healing. Nevertheless, he was miraculously healed through the faith of an intermediary.

The third agent of faith is the person who does the healing. Unless we read things into the text that are not here, the most reasonable conclusion is that the agents of faith for the healing of the lame beggar were Peter and John.[2]

Wagner notes that in at least one of the New Testament miracles there is no evidence that the recipient was a believer. This was the case when the lame beggar was healed; the man had shown no sign of faith in either Jesus or divine healing. Yet in other cases, such as those involving the two blind men, Jesus asked the recipients of the miracles to first affirm that they believed He had the power to heal them (see Matt. 9:27-31).

FIVE PRINCIPLES OF FAITH

Since my own healing of allergies and since the days I prayed for many people to be healed at TAG meetings, I watch in wonder at what God does, and I also study His actions. I look for consistencies from which we might be able to draw principles. Again, what I lay out here is not a formula, nor is it a panacea; rather, it is a model, or standard, from which we can learn in order to discover more power in healing.

Through my observations, I have been able to glean five basic principles of faith as they apply to healing. The basis for these principles is found in Mark 11:22-24:

"Have faith in God," Jesus answered. "I tell you the truth, if anyone says to this mountain, 'Go, throw yourself into the sea,' and does not doubt in his heart but believes that what he says will happen, it will be done for him. Therefore I tell you, whatever you ask for in prayer, believe that you have received it, and it will be yours."

1. Faith Is Relational

Jesus said, "Have faith in God" (Mark 11:22). He does not say to have faith in faith or to have faith primarily in God's Word; He made it clear that we are to have faith in a Person. God wants us to have a personal relationship with Him in which we trust in His love and His faithful character. The writer of Hebrews emphasizes that faith in God is foundational for every believer:

> Therefore let us leave the elementary teachings about Christ and go on to maturity, not laying again the foundation of repentance from acts that lead to death, and of faith in God (Heb. 6:1).

When my children were young, one of their favorite games was to jump off the bed and shout, "Catch me, Daddy!" Of course I would catch them. My kids had faith in me, in my faithfulness as a father. Even as my children have grown older, they still have faith in me. My son celebrated a birthday during the time when I was writing this book. It was important to him that I spend an afternoon with him to celebrate this special day. I gave my word that I would, and I did. Of course I enjoy spending time with my son, but when I am busy it's not always easy to find the time. Yet my son had faith that I would follow through. God wants this same kind of childlike faith directed toward Him when it comes to healing. What parent doesn't want to see his or her sick child well again? If we as imperfect parents want to see our children healed of sicknesses, how much more does our good heavenly Father, perfect in love, desire our well-being?

Many times when I pray for someone, I intercede for that person by appealing to the Father heart of God. God is a personal, loving Father who is interested in every aspect of our lives. I have learned that He is interested in what I think, how I feel and what pains I am suffering. He wants me to go to Him in prayer with both big and small things.

I discovered this truth as a young Christian. One day while driving with one hand on the wheel, I chewed absentmindedly at a fingernail on my other hand. Since I was focused on the road, I inadvertently peeled a sliver of skin from the side of my nail. The pain was excruciating, and I immediately berated myself for my stupidity. It hurt so much that I was ready to pray to be healed then and there!

But a thought stopped me: *This is such a small thing! I don't want to bother God with my little problem. There are people suffering much greater things than my hanging skin.* Inwardly, I seemed to hear God say, *Son, I love you; and even if you are hurting with a minor injury, I am concerned and I want to heal you.* I didn't know if they were my thoughts or God's, so I decided to pray and see if God really had been speaking. I figured that if I got healed, then God had spoken to me; so I prayed.

Immediately the pain left, and I was totally healed. Out loud I confessed, "Jesus, you are so marvelous! You are interested in the little things in my life." I was young then, but I have seen God confirm over and over how faithful He is.

Here is another example of something little yet very

important to God: Jack Richardson was attending a Vineyard conference in Atlanta but was unable to concentrate at the beginning—he had a pounding headache, and aspirin did not even put a dent into it. He was at the conference with people from his home church in Florida, and they had been learning how to step out in faith. One of his friends took the initiative and placed his hands on Jack's head, asking God to remove the headache so that Jack could fully participate in the conference and become a better Christian. Nothing happened. It was as if God were saying, "Not yet. I have a lesson for you to learn."

Jack and his friend realized at the same time that they were trying to manipulate God into taking away the headache. His friend again placed his hands on Jack's head and said, "God, You love Jack. We know that You want Him to be whole. By the healing power of Your Holy Spirit, we ask that You clear Jack's head and take away the pain." Two seconds later, the headache was gone and did not return for the duration of the conference. The test here was for Jack and his friend to see that they did not have to twist God's arm; rather, God loved Jack and wanted to heal him.

This is the type of relationship Abraham had with God. Abraham believed God, and "he considered him faithful who had made the promise" (Heb. 11:11). And that is the kind of relationship He wants with each of us. We can trust Him with our sicknesses, big or small, because He is so in love with us and cares for us!

2. Faith Is Revelational

Let's again look at the second part of the passage in Mark 11. Jesus says:

I tell you the truth, if anyone says to this mountain, "Go, throw yourself into the sea," and does not doubt in his heart but believes that what he says will happen, it will be done for him (v. 23).

I live near Pasadena, California. Every day (when it is not too smoggy) I can look out at the San Gabriel Mountains and Mount Wilson, which gloriously rises 5,700 feet above sea level. Not a behemoth when it comes to the world's tallest peaks, but it is nonetheless substantial. As tempting as it might be, I do not think that I have ever thought of telling Mount Wilson to move. It would be foolhardy to command it or any mountain to be thrown into the sea, unless of course, we have heard from God. Even then, I think I might want to start with a smaller mountain—or maybe a hill or a pile of rocks.

Our human inclination is to start small and, if that works, inch our way up. However, God does not necessarily work that way. He is more interested in the faith to move the mountain than the size of the mountain to be moved. Thus, faith is released as we receive revelation from His Word. This is why Romans 10:17 declares, "Consequently, faith comes from hearing the message, and the message is heard through the word of Christ."

Two Greek words, *logos* and *rhema,* are translated into English as "word." "Logos" is the written Word; "rhema" is the revelatory word, the word that imparts faith. "Word" in Romans 10:17 is "rhema." So when we read or hear God's rhema, faith to activate the healing results. Many times I will lay hands on the sick and quote Mark 16:18, which promises that we will lay hands on the sick and they will recover. But I always ask the person, "Do you believe the Word?" I don't want him or her just to receive the biblical promise intellectually; rather, I want the person to have faith in God's Word. By asking that question, the written logos becomes the revelatory rhema, and many receive healing.

I also give words of knowledge whenever I pray for the sick. Words of knowledge are bestowed when the Holy Spirit imparts information, or knowledge, about the condition of sick people. When words of knowledge are given, people's faith is released, and many receive their healing as they receive these words.

I have given thousands of words, and I believe that more people are healed this way than by simply laying hands on them and praying. Now, I have to admit that if you came to one of my healing services, you would not find the words to be that impressive. I am not a prophet, and I do not normally give very specific words concerning a person's sickness. It was said that William Branham, a healing evangelist of the late 1940s and 1950s, would call people out by name and he would miraculously receive the names of specific diseases people had—then they would be healed. My words are general. I usually say something like "There is someone who is being healed of asthma and allergies." This is similar to what Benny Hinn did at the meeting in Hollywood, although he did have a few more specifics, such as knowing which ear needed healing.

I'm sure that those who are critical of this method of healing would argue that in a group of any size, the odds are good that someone present has asthma or allergies. I agree. But this is not how I approach giving words of knowledge. I don't go into a meeting thinking, *Well, the odds are good that people with back problems will be there. So I'll say it and maybe someone will believe the word and get healed.* Instead, I listen in prayer while I am giving the words. And whatever words of different sicknesses I receive, I speak them in faith. The words may be general, but God moves and people get healed.

Take for example a healing service in Australia where I was speaking. I gave a word about a person with carpal tunnel syndrome. I described a person who had sharp pain from the hands up to the arms and into the neck. A woman came forward to testify that she had had carpal tunnel syndrome for more than two years. She had gone to numerous healing services, and not one person had ever given a word of knowledge concerning this problem. The word God had given me was specific, as she indeed suffered from pain that went all the way up her arm into her neck. When I gave the word, she was instantly healed. The point of this word, like all others I give, is not to focus on what God does through me or to build up a list of healing testimonies under my ministry or to establish any kind of mystique. To the contrary, the purpose is to build and release faith in the person who is to be healed. Jesus is so wonderful! He knows our problems and wants us to be restored to full health.

3. Faith Is Risky

When Jesus suggests that we throw a mountain into the sea by faith, He is using hyperbole to make the point that faith always believes God can do the impossible. We have to step out in faith, and then God will back us up. I heard it said this way: We do the ridiculous and God will do the miraculous.

The Bible overflows with examples of this principle. Peter was commanded to walk on the water. He took a risk: He stepped out of his boat, and God backed him up. It was only as Peter began to look around and recognize the seeming impossibility of walking on water that he started to sink (see Matt. 14:25-30).

Blind Bartimaeus took a major risk by screaming for Jesus

to have mercy on him. Even though he was rebuked, he per-sisted. When Jesus called for him, he threw away his cloak. For beggars, their cloaks were indispensable, as they were their shelter when they slept. By throwing away the cloak, Bartimaeus was saying, "I'm not going to need this ever again because Jesus is going to heal me." Faith was risky for Bartimaeus, but God backed him up (see Mark 10:46-52).

The leper and the woman with the issue of blood took major risks by publicly approaching Jesus, even though the Mosaic Law commanded that they remain quarantined. They stepped out in faith and were rewarded by complete and instantaneous healing (see Matt. 8:2-3; 9:20-22).

I know that whenever I conduct a healing service, I'm tak-ing a risk. There are times that I have stepped out to pray for the sick and to give words of knowledge, only to hear silence when I ask if anyone has been healed. But my conviction is to continue to pray for the sick in public, because the more I step out in faith, the more I see dramatic healings. Besides, Jesus is the Healer; I believe that as I do what seems ridiculous, He will do the miraculous. It is up to Him, not me.

The healing I wrote about in chapter 4 is a perfect example of stepping out in faith. I took a huge risk when I told a seem-ingly barren woman that she would have a baby within one year, but I wanted to remain faithful to the word of knowledge I felt I was receiving. God backed me up, however, for the woman returned the next month saying she was three weeks pregnant!

I have heard it said often and have witnessed its truth in real life: faith is spelled r-i-s-k! The Yiddish word for the nerve to take a risk is chutzpah. Louie is someone who had chutz-pah, but he lost something else: the tip of his right index finger. It had been accidentally severed when he and his stepdaughter were in their yard cutting branches. Though he was rushed to the hospital, doctors were unable to reattach the tip.

Louie and his family had been attending Harvest Rock Church and were present the Sunday after the accident. After the service he asked me to pray for him: "I believe God wants to heal me, to grow this finger out." Since Louie was taking a risk and God wants to heal people, I had to push aside my doubts. I touched Louie's hand and spoke a brief prayer of agreement. Nothing dramatic happened, and I moved on to the next person who was seeking prayer.

Doctors had told Louie that his finger would always be just a stump. Yet over a period of weeks Louie and his family watched in amazement as a bit of nail appeared on his finger and then grew to within an eighth of an inch of its original length. A hand specialist suggested that perhaps there were some cells that were not damaged and were able to regenerate themselves. Louie, however, had taken a risk of faith and knew God had healed him.

4. Faith Is Real

Hebrews 11:1 declares, "Now faith is being sure of what we hope for and certain of what we do not see." In other words, faith is now. It is having what we're believing for now. In our spirit, we know that we have it now. We believe we are healed now.

Look again at Mark 11:22-24. It is clear that first we have to believe and then we will receive. Jesus said, "Believe that you have received it, and it will be yours" (v. 24). The tendency in the world is to say, "First receive, then believe"; but this is not how God's kingdom principle of faith works.

I learned this lesson right after my wife, Sue, and I were married. We went to see a movie produced by WorldWide Pictures—

Billy Graham's film production company. It featured Graham speaking at a crusade and was being shown as an outreach in our home church. About halfway through the movie, my lower jaw locked, and I felt excruciating pain shoot from one side of my jaw to the other. It hurt, and it was scary. I couldn't open or close my jaw, not even slightly. I rushed out of the auditorium to the men's room, immediately praying over my jaw.

On this occasion, nothing happened. I tried to manipulate my jaw with my hands, but it remained stubbornly locked. Finally, I went into the auditorium and explained to Sue through clenched jaws that we had to leave. The next morning, there was some mobility of the jaw, but I still could not open my mouth more than three-quarters of an inch. The shooting pains were still unbearable.

My brother-in-law is a doctor. In fact, he is an ear, nose and throat specialist, so I set up an appointment to find out what exactly was going on. After he examined me, he opined, "I think you have TMJ."

I replied, "What is TMJ?"

"It is arthritis of the jaw. Further, there is no real cure for it. But just to make sure, there is a specialist in my hospital who specializes in TMJ, and I'll call him to take a look at you just to get a confirmation."

A week later I saw the specialist, and he confirmed what my brother-in-law had said. Yep, I had TMJ.

"Is there anything I can do? Can surgery fix it?" I pleaded.

"No, not really. Surgery is really complex when it comes to TMJ. Most times the surgery does more harm than good. You just have to live with it. I recommend that you just take Advil," he said.

"You mean take Advil for the rest of my life?"

"That is the best advice I can give you."

As these words fell from the lips of the specialist, some-thing rose up within my spirit and I told myself, *I refuse that advice. I refuse to take Advil for the rest of my life. And further, I refuse to have TMJ for the rest of my life.*

I knew that this affliction was not of God, since I knew he had called me to preach. With TMJ, I could hardly speak, let

> # WE CANNOT ALLOW
> # WHAT WE SEE OR FEEL TO
> # SHAKE OUR FAITH.

alone *preach!* Besides, I had been eating soft food since the TMJ symptoms first appeared; and I knew there was no way I could go through life not eating my favorite foods—ribs and steak. (This might have been the greater bummer at that point in my life.)

I truly wanted the normal use of my jaw back, so I made a covenant with God. Every time I saw myself in the mirror, I would confess Mark 11:23 and would say, "Father, I want to thank You in advance; I believe that I have received my heal-ing!"

We all see ourselves in a mirror several times throughout any given day. We get a glance when we wake up, each time we go to the rest room, when we put on makeup in the car (if we are women), when we try on a new shirt at the department store and when we brush our teeth before going to bed. Each time I saw myself, I said, "Father, thank You. I believe that I have received my healing!" I repeated this even though there was no change in my physical condition. But I have learned that faith is now. It is real. We have to believe first; then we receive. We cannot allow what we see or feel to shake our faith.

700 Club host and Christian Broadcasting Network president Pat Robertson explains this dynamic wonderfully:

> In our spirits, we must always see God. In God there is no sickness, no failure, no defeat, no problem. Our mouths must declare our victory in God. If we do that, we will see victory.
>
> I do not mean that you should ignore material reality. Sickness and suffering are real, but God's reality is greater. For example, let's assume you had an accident in which your leg is broken. You can say, "I broke my leg. It hurts. But God's power is healing my leg right now. The pain is leaving. Jesus is doing a miracle, and I thank Him for it. I thank Him that regardless of what happened to my leg, a miracle is taking place. Therefore I command my leg to knit together and be healed. Praise God!" This type of confession will mobilize spiritual power toward healing and victory.
>
> But suppose instead you say after the accident, "Oh, I can't stand the pain! It's the most horrible pain I've ever had! It will take a long time. My leg may never be healed." That negative confession admits defeat and directs the flow of spiritual power to ensure a long and painful convalescence.[3]

Dodie Osteen, who cofounded and copastored Lakewood Church in Houston, Texas, with her late husband, John, took this principle to the ultimate test when some years ago she was diagnosed with cancer. In the book *Healed of Cancer*, Mrs. Osteen tells of her struggle with this life-threatening disease. She had her husband take authority over the sickness, claiming that it would not lead to death. He anointed her with oil; then, in the days that followed, she began to claim the Word of God.

> In spite of every discouraging symptom, my heart knew that God's Word could not lie. I had confidence in God's Word. If I hadn't, I would have died. Hebrews 10:23 says, "Let us hold fast the confession of our hope without wavering, for He who promised is faithful."[4]

From Proverbs 4:20-23 to John 10:10 to Revelation 12:11, Mrs. Osteen daily confessed Scripture—40 of them specific to healing. She has done this for years. "I know I am healed," she writes. "I left the hospital December 10, 1981, and today, I am still alive, full of energy, and very active. . . . The fact that I am still living is a pretty good indication that the Word of God works."[5] Years later, Mrs. Osteen had blood work done that confirmed the miracle.

That's wonderful, you might say, but what happened to the TMJ? Well, to make a long story short, more than a year went by after that fateful night in the auditorium when I watched the Billy Graham movie. Each day, I quoted Scripture, expecting to see a miracle. One day, just like every other day, I woke up and greeted the morning with a yawn— but on this morning I was able to open my jaw fully! I had been totally healed of my TMJ; complete mobility had been restored and I felt absolutely no pain. I have been healed ever since.

5. Faith Is Resolute

> Therefore I tell you, whatever you ask for in prayer,
> believe that you have received it, and it will be yours
> (Mark 11:24).

The text doesn't give any timetable as to when we will receive the answer to our prayers. What is implied, however, is that we continue believing God's Word, as Dodie Osteen did, even if we don't receive the manifestation of the healing or if we receive only a partial manifestation. Jesus taught us that we should "always pray and not give up" (Luke 18:1).

I once heard a story of a respected healing evangelist who prayed for a blind person at his healing crusade. Nothing happened. But the evangelist encouraged the blind person to continue believing regardless of the circumstances. Three years later, as this blind person was getting his hair cut at a barbershop, he suddenly could see clearly and completely.

Pat Boone's adult grandson is another example. In June 2001, Ryan Corbin fell three stories, landing on a cement slab. He had a serious head injury and was unconscious. Doctors hinted that the family might want to think about pulling the plug. Ryan's father, Doug Corbin, would not hear of it. He declared that the doctors were a good medical team and had saved Ryan's life, but that the Boone family was a good faith team.

For most of the first year, Ryan was in a partial coma and largely unresponsive, but his family never gave up. Finally, on what had been a typical visit, Ryan ate pudding spoon-fed to him by his sister, Jessica. Despite the doctor's predictions that he would never be a productive member of society, today Ryan has moved back home, can talk some, can go to church and sing and is improving each day. It is a healing in progress.

What does Ryan say about it? When asked if he will be completely healed, without hesitation Ryan responds in the affirmative and declares it will be "for the glory of God."[6]

I don't understand the reasons behind God's choosing to heal at certain times and not others, but my posture and conviction is this: If I am sick, I am going to persevere and believe God for the healing until the healing comes, regardless of the timing. And I would much rather die having believed and not received than to go through life having thrown in the towel through unbelief and doubt.

After all, the Bible declares that many ancients of old themselves did not live to witness the manifestation of the promises God had made to them. Nevertheless, they were commended for their faith (see Heb. 11:39).

START BELIEVING NOW

Let me encourage you to start believing in God's Word and in His character. Start believing that you have your healing now, even if it takes a year (as I experienced) or possibly even longer (as Ryan Corbin is experiencing) before you actually receive it. This leads me to the last point I want to make in this chapter: We need to persevere in our fight of faith.

In the end, we are here to please and glorify God. The Bible declares that "without faith it is impossible to please God" (Heb. 11:6). Therefore, continue to persevere in your faith; whether or not you receive your healing in this life, your reward will be great in heaven.

Notes

1. Chuck D. Pierce and Robert Heidler, *Restoring Your Shield of Faith* (Ventura, CA: Regal Books, 2004).

2. C. Peter Wagner, *Acts of the Holy Spirit* (Ventura, CA: Regal Books, 1994), p. 93.

3. Pat Robertson, "Pat's Perspective—Kingdom Power," *CBN.org*, 2003. http://cbn.org/spirituallife%2Fholyspirit%2Fpat's_perspective_kingdom_power.asp (accessed August 25, 2003).

4. Dodie Osteen, *Healed of Cancer* (Houston, TX: John Osteen Publications, 1986), p. 24.

5. Ibid., pp. 36-37.

6. Ryan Corbin, quoted in Steven Lawson, "A Miracle for Ryan," *Charisma* (June 2003), p. 78.

Chapter 6

THE WHY-BAD-THINGS-HAPPEN-TO-GOOD-PEOPLE FACTOR

Sin and Satan work disorder and destruction. God doesn't. He shows us how to surmount our heartbreaks and our tendency to fail, and helps us to overcome the slings of satanic fury bent on death and destruction.

JACK HAYFORD, "HEALING FOR TODAY," *LIVINGWAY.ORG*

Why will Lucy easily catch a cold but Stephanie will not? Why did Mr. Jones have a heart attack but his neighbor, Mr. Smith, did not? Why do many sexually active teens contract HIV but others do not? Each of these is a variation of the perplexing question CNN talk show host Larry King often asks: Why do bad things happen to good people?

The question here is not, Will God heal? or Why do some people receive healing when others do not? The dilemma is, Why do some people get sick and others do not? After all, if we do not get sick, then we do not need to be healed. So what is the cause of illness? Old age? Carelessness? The devil?

A plethora of answers will arise as we investigate someone's illness or ask why someone else never got sick. Some of the reasons will be obvious. Libby got the flu because she carpooled with Amy, who just got over the flu. Other reasons will not be so obvious. Mike got skin cancer, yet he never goes to the beach and has seldom been exposed to the sun. Worse yet, Ethan is in a coma after the car he was riding in was struck by a drunk driver.

Often after asking why, the next question is, Whose sin was it? The person's who is sick? His parents'? Her husband's? The drunk driver's? Adam's? Everybody's? Nobody's?

If we look on the surface, the reason may or may not be apparent. After all, the rain does fall on the just and the unjust alike. However, if we look more closely, we will find a root cause behind most sickness or physical problems.

THE ROOT CAUSE

While not all sickness is a direct result of a specific sin, the root issue of sin can be the culprit. The root issue of sin not only opens the door for sickness but can also prevent people from receiving healing.

Not a Rule

Before I continue, though, I must stress that *not all* sickness comes as a result of one's sin. Other causes of sickness are operative, such as physiological laws, accidents or the simple fact that we live in a fallen world.

My mother passed away in May 2003. She had received tainted blood during a blood transfusion that led to hepatitis

> THE ROOT ISSUE OF SIN NOT ONLY OPENS THE DOOR FOR SICKNESS BUT CAN ALSO PREVENT PEOPLE FROM RECEIVING HEALING.

C and then liver cancer, which eventually caused her death. This was, I believe, a tragic accident and *not* the result of sin on my mother's part.

Likewise, we must be cautious when we see situations such as the great tragedy in Singapore. One Christian woman contracted SARS while she was visiting China. When she returned home to Singapore, she was hospitalized. Her pastor, family and friends visited her and prayed for her recovery. She did recover, but her pastor and several family members also contracted SARS and they died. How was sin involved here? We do not know the details of the spiritual lives of these people, but it certainly appears that no one person's overt sin caused this tragedy. Of course, there was the overarching effect of living in a fallen world that allows such misfortune to occur, but that is quite different from an individual's sin resulting in sickness.

Jack Hayford, the respected pastor emeritus of The Church On The Way in Van Nuys, California, puts it this way:

I believe in the power of God's Word and Spirit to sustain and supply health to those who walk simply and humbly before Him in faith. I believe the fruit of such faith will be manifest in love and patience.

So I reject any system that produces lovelessness or induces guilt when a believer in Jesus does not seem to be able to receive physical healing or personal deliverance from sickness or any other torment.[1]

Charles Kraft adds this caution:

If we trace the issues that give the Enemy rights to inhabit us, sin would probably underlie every one of them, simply because of the fallen world we live in and our fallen nature. The satanic kingdom, however, specializes in accusing people and getting them to blame themselves for much that is not their fault. Undeserved guilt, then, becomes a major avenue for demonization. And one of the spinoffs of this is the self-blame that many feel for being demonized. We must, therefore, be very careful when we are dealing with hurting people who often live under a load of condemnation lest we unwittingly add to their guilt and thus to the grip the Enemy has on them. . . . Remember that if it is not loving, it is not God's way.[2]

Wise words from wise men.

I share the stories of my mother and the pastor in Singapore so that if a reader is fighting sickness and does not sense any unconfessed sin in his or her life, he or she will not feel condemned or become overly introspective. I also refer back to the introduction: All healing, including the causes and effects of it, is ultimately a mystery.

I have seen situations in which God healed the sinners in a sovereign way without any prior repentance. In one such case, a man I knew was leading a double life. He was ready to leave his wife and children for another woman when he had an accident at work. He broke his arm and burned his hand severely. He was backslidden, and yet God healed him when his Christian friends prayed for him. If I were God, I would have let him suffer for his immorality (aren't you glad that God is God and we are not?). But that is the mystery of healing.

The Root and the Fruit

Even with the mystery that envelops healing, there are sufficient scriptural principles to help us see that sin is a root issue of sickness. If we deal with the root, we will see the fruit—healing.

The Bible contains many verses that illustrate the relationship between sin and sickness. James 5:14-16 reads:

> Is any one of you sick? He should call the elders of the church to pray over him and anoint him with oil in the name of the Lord. And the prayer offered in faith will make the sick person well; the Lord will raise him up. If he has sinned, he will be forgiven. *Therefore confess your sins to each other and pray for each other so that you may be healed.* The prayer of a righteous man is powerful and effective (emphasis added).

Psalm 32:1-5 reads:

> Blessed is he whose transgressions are forgiven,

whose sins are covered. Blessed is the man whose sin the LORD does not count against him and in whose spirit is no deceit. When I kept silent, my bones wasted away through my groaning all day long. For day and night your hand was heavy upon me; my strength was sapped as in the heat of summer. . . . Then I acknowledged my sin to you and did not cover up my iniquity. I said, "I will confess my transgressions to the LORD"—and you forgave the guilt of my sin.

I wonder if David suffered from osteoporosis, a disease causing bone brittleness, because of his sins. What did he mean when he said, "My bones wasted away"? Regardless of David's actual affliction, when he kept his sins covered, he suffered physical illness.

David went on to say:

Because of your wrath there is no health in my body; my bones have no soundness because of my sin. My guilt has overwhelmed me like a burden too heavy to bear. My wounds fester and are loathsome because of my sinful folly. I am bowed down and brought very low; all day long I go about mourning. My back is filled with searing pain; there is no health in my body. I am feeble and utterly crushed; I groan in anguish of heart (Ps. 38:3-8).

In verses 10, 17 and 18, he continued, "My heart pounds, my strength fails me; even the light has gone from my eyes. For I am about to fall, and my pain is ever with me. I confess my iniquity; I am troubled by my sin."

Deuteronomy 28:58-61 lists the curses of disobedience:

> If you do not carefully follow all the words of this law,
> which are written in this book, and do not revere this
> glorious and awesome name—the LORD your God—
> the LORD will send fearful plagues on you and your
> descendants, harsh and prolonged disasters, and
> severe and lingering illnesses. He will bring upon you
> all the diseases of Egypt that you dreaded, and they
> will cling to you. The LORD will also bring on you
> every kind of sickness and disaster not recorded in this
> Book of the Law, until you are destroyed.

I understand this to mean that when we sin, we open the door
for physical judgment, often manifested in "severe and linger-
ing illnesses."

Yet when we repent of our sins, God often heals.

> Praise the LORD, O my soul; all my inmost being,
> praise his holy name. Praise the LORD, O my soul, and
> forget not all his benefits—who forgives all your sins
> and heals all your diseases, who redeems your life from
> the pit and crowns you with love and compassion (Ps.
> 103:1-4).

It is interesting to note that when Jesus healed the paralytic man, He first dealt with the root issue of sin before he pro-
nounced the healing:

> Jesus stepped into a boat, crossed over and came to his
> own town. Some men brought to him a paralytic, lying
> on a mat. When Jesus saw their faith, he said to the

paralytic, "Take heart, son; your sins are forgiven." At this, some of the teachers of the law said to themselves, "This fellow is blaspheming!" Knowing their thoughts, Jesus said, "Why do you entertain evil thoughts in your hearts? Which is easier: to say, 'Your sins are forgiven,' or to say, 'Get up and walk'? But so that you may know that the Son of Man has authority on earth to forgive sins. . . ." Then he said to the paralytic, "Get up, take your mat and go home." And the man got up and went home (Matt. 9:1-7).

Jesus was not sidetracked by the accusation of blasphemy. His intention was to heal the paralytic, but He dealt with the root issue of sin before He could pronounce the healing.

Another time, at the pool of Bethesda, after healing a man who had been paralyzed for 38 years, Jesus told the man, "See, you are well again. Stop sinning or something worse may happen to you" (John 5:14). Apparently, sinning can incur something worse than being unable to move around for almost half a century.

I respect what Billy Graham says about sin in his classic book *Peace With God:*

The most devastating fact in the universe is sin. The cause of all troubles, the root of all sorrow, the dread of every man lies in this one small word sin. All mental disorders, all sicknesses, all destruction, all wars find their root in sin. Sin is madness in the brain, poison in the heart. It is a tornado on the loose, a volcano gone wild. It is a deadly cancer eating its way into the souls of men. It is a raging torrent that sweeps everything before it.[3]

Francis MacNutt puts it this way:

> Our physical sickness, far from being a redemptive blessing, is often a sign that we are not redeemed, not whole on a spiritual level.[4]

Medical Proof

Sin as a cause of sickness is confirmed in the medical community. In 1998, the John Templeton Foundation sponsored a symposium of leading doctors at Duke Medical School, chaired by Dr. Harold Koenig, professor of psychiatry and medicine and director of the Center for the Study of Religion/Spirituality and Health at Duke Medical Center. The focus of this symposium was psychoneuroimmunology, a term coined to show the relationship among the mind, the brain and the immune system. *John Templeton Magazine* summed up the findings:

> Do anger, guilt, anxiety, helplessness, or isolation have a corresponding negative effect on our ability to deal with physical, emotional or social stress? A rapidly growing body of research suggests that these connections are far more important than traditional Western medical science had previously supposed. One interesting result of this relatively new line of inquiry is the indication that personal faith and religious practice may be associated with a positive immune function and response to stress.[5]

This conclusion in the medical community that faith improves one's immune system while negative emotions make a person more susceptible to illness only confirms the biblical principle.

LOOK AT THE SPIRITUAL AND PHYSIOLOGICAL CONNECTION

It is clear that sin does indeed have an impact upon us physically. Below are five examples of sin's effects, both spiritual and physiological, on the human race:

1. Sin causes stress. Stress breaks down our natural immune system.
2. Sin causes us to feel guilt. Guilt breaks down our immune system.
3. In the spiritual realm, sin gives Satan a legal right to attack us and our children.
4. Sin can open the door for demonization and cause greater sickness.[6]
5. Sin hinders prayers, so people are not healed.

Dear God, give me the wisdom to discern when Satan tells a lie about my physical condition or the sickness of someone else. Give me the ability to love in all situations and to recognize and cut off the root cause of illness—which is sin. Forgive me and make me whole this day. In Jesus' name, amen.

Notes

1. Jack Hayford, "Healing for Today," *Jack Hayford Ministries,* July 9, 2003. http://www.livingway.org/articles/Healing_Today.htm (accessed September 2, 2003).
2. Charles H. Kraft, *Deep Wounds, Deep Healing* (Ann Arbor, MI: Servant Publications, 1993), p. 264.
3. Billy Graham, *Peace With God: The Secret of Happiness* (Nashville, TN: Word Publishing, 2000), n.p.
4. Francis MacNutt, *Healing* (Notre Dame, IN: Ave Maria Press, 1974), n.p.
5. *John Templeton Magazine* (n.p.), p. 5.
6. For more on how sin opens the door to demonization, read Charles H. Kraft, *Deep Wounds, Deep Healing* (Ann Arbor, MI: Servant Publications, 1993), pp. 255-274.

Chapter 7

THE SIN FACTOR

God has not promised to destroy the works of the devil in our bodies
while we are clinging to the works of the devil in our souls.
F. F. BOSWORTH, *CHRIST THE HEALER*

Over the years, I have prayed for literally thousands of people
with myriad ailments and pains. During this time in the
healing ministry, I have observed five major types of sin that
are root causes of sickness. I'm sure that this is a partial list,
but it has proven helpful to me and to many others when trying to understand the relationship among sin, sickness and
healing.

1. SINS OF EMOTION AND ATTITUDE

Unbelief and pride are two sides of the same coin. Each can easily arise in minds and hearts—after all, we are all too human. The Bible clearly cautions against unbelief (which is the opposite of belief and which dismisses the truth) and pride (which is exalting ourselves, our opinions and our actions). There are many emotions and attitudes that affect our walks with God and many that can hinder healing, but unbelief and pride seem to be particularly effective at stemming God's working in our lives and His making us whole.

Unbelief

In chapter 5, I wrote about the role and importance of faith in healing. Now I want to focus on unbelief, which in reality is sin. Romans 14:23 reads, "And everything that does not come from faith is sin." In fact, Hebrews 3:12 (*NKJV*) calls it "an evil heart of unbelief."

Fear is a manifestation of unbelief. Second Timothy 1:7 makes this clear: "For God did not give us a spirit of timidity, but a spirit of power, of love and of self-discipline." Another form of unbelief may be anxiety, which reveals a heart that does not fully trust God's sovereignty. Philippians 4:6-7 reads, "Do not be anxious about anything, but in everything, by prayer and petition, with thanksgiving, present your requests to God."

These sins are critical to recognize, and it is essential to deal with them not only because they open the door for sickness but also because they are huge obstacles when it comes to being healed. Fear and anxiety can bring so much stress to an individual that his or her immune system is violated, opening the door for sickness. God is not pleased, nor will He honor our requests, when we pray for our healing in an atmosphere of doubt and unbelief (see Heb. 11:6). To the contrary, we are to expect a miracle.

One way we demonstrate our belief is by confession. By this I mean, if we confess Christ as our Savior and declare His good works, then we are demonstrating what we believe. Of course, our actions must match our words.

The healing evangelist F. F. Bosworth made this point clear in his classic book *Christ the Healer*:

> We never rise above our confession. A negative confession will lower us to the level of that confession. It is what we confess with our lips that really controls us. Our confession imprisons us if it is negative, or sets us free if it is positive. . . . Confessing a lack of faith increases doubt. Every time you confess doubts and fears, you confess your faith in Satan and deny the ability and grace of God.[1]

Bosworth is not saying that Satan has more power than God. To the contrary, he is explaining the biblical principle of the power of our words and attitudes, a freedom that God has given us and that can have grave consequences if not properly used.

Belief, then, is important in receiving a healing. However, this is not to say that God only heals those who believe He can heal. While unbelief can at times keep us from being healed, God always has the power to heal people despite their unbelief.

Pride

Another sin that I have seen that opens the door to sickness is what I call pride, or an orientation toward performance. The Bible declares that when we move in pride and selfish ambition, we invite demonic activity into our lives.

But if you harbor bitter envy and selfish ambition in your hearts, do not boast about it or deny the truth. Such "wisdom" does not come down from heaven but is earthly, unspiritual, of the devil. For where you have envy and selfish ambition, there you find disorder and every evil practice (Jas. 3:14-16).

I have noticed that many people who have problems with scoliosis come from performance-oriented homes. By this I

> WHILE UNBELIEF CAN AT TIMES KEEP US FROM BEING HEALED, GOD ALWAYS HAS THE POWER TO HEAL PEOPLE DESPITE THEIR UNBELIEF.

mean that the parents have high expectations and make judgments of personal value based primarily or solely on accomplishments. I have noticed this to be particularly true in Asian homes. There is so much pressure on the children to achieve academically that this stress sometimes results in scoliosis. This particular form of scoliosis, more a muscular condition than a skeletal one, is exacerbated by stress. I have seen many people deal with the root issue of performance orientation (a manifestation of pride) by repenting, and then they receive healing from scoliosis.

Sometimes the stress is self-imposed. For example, there was a period of time when my daughter, Grace, had scoliosis. When we as parents repented of any performance orientation that we had imposed upon her and she, in turn, repented of the stress she had imposed upon herself through her own drive to achieve, her muscles began to relax and her back soon straightened out.

Others have suffered heart problems due to strife and ambition. When they repent of these offenses, God begins to heal their cardiac problems.

Evidence is overwhelming that stress breaks down the immune system. If we find that our immune system is weak, it could mean that we are striving in pride, slaves of our performance-oriented lives. Repent of such actions and attitudes and believe God to heal you physically.

(Note: This does not mean that all heart problems or stress problems are related to pride, but if a person has such a condition, looking at the level of pride in his or her life is a good place to begin.)

2. Sins We Commit Against Others

All sins are committed against God, but they come in many shapes and forms. We all commit sins against other people, in the Church in particular and in society in general. The Bible is clear that if there is division within a church, it opens the door for not only sickness but also premature death. Consider the warning in 1 Corinthians 11:27-31:

Therefore, whoever eats the bread or drinks the cup of the Lord in an unworthy manner will be guilty of sinning against the body and blood of the Lord. A man ought to examine himself before he eats of the bread and drinks of the cup. For anyone who eats and drinks without recognizing the body of the Lord eats and drinks judgment on himself. That is why many among you are weak and sick, and a number of you have fallen asleep. But if we judged ourselves, we would not come under judgment.

I have found that cancer can sometimes be traced to a divisive, independent spirit. This doesn't happen all the time; in fact, the root cause of some cancer is environmental, like cigarette smoking. And as I have already shared, my mother developed liver cancer from a blood transfusion that was contaminated with hepatitis C. However, when there is no environmental root cause, I would suggest that the inflicted person ask if he or she has been divisive and independent in the Body of Christ. The parallel here is that cancer cells are cells that decide to rebel. If we are struggling with bitterness or judgment toward others in the Body of Christ, I strongly recommend that at the very least, we do not dishonor God by partaking of the Lord's Supper. According to the way I read 1 Corinthians 11:27-31, we are opening the door to sickness. Better yet, let's repent of the judgment and forgive from our heart.

This suggestion is made with the best of intentions and with the full realization that cancer research is ongoing. When someone has cancer, we should never judge them as having sinned. While there can be a cause-and-effect relationship, there also may be other explanations, as I have already noted. As we would with anyone who is ill, we should love the cancer patient and pray for healing.

There are other root sins that we commit against others that possibly cause sickness in our body. Let's look at some attitudes that can rip us apart emotionally, socially and even physically.

Bitterness

Hebrews 12:15 explains, "See to it that no one misses the grace of God and that no bitter root grows up to cause trouble and defile many." We see how bitterness can cause trouble and defile us and others.

Repeatedly, Jesus commands us to forgive and then promises that we will be forgiven (see Matt. 6:12-14; 18:21-22; Mark 11:25; Luke 11:4; 17:4; John 20:23). Jesus taught that if we do not forgive, we will be handed over to the tormentors. The seriousness of not forgiving is illustrated by the parable of the unmerciful servant, found in Matthew 18:22-35:

> Jesus answered, "I tell you, [you must forgive] not seven times, but seventy-seven times.
>
> "Therefore, the kingdom of heaven is like a king who wanted to settle accounts with his servants. As he began the settlement, a man who owed him ten thousand talents was brought to him. Since he was not able to pay, the master ordered that he and his wife and his children and all that he had be sold to repay the debt.
>
> "The servant fell on his knees before him. 'Be patient with me,' he begged, 'and I will pay back everything.' The servant's master took pity on him, canceled the debt and let him go.
>
> "But when that servant went out, he found one of his fellow servants who owed him a hundred denarii. He grabbed him and began to choke him. 'Pay back what you owe me!' he demanded.
>
> "His fellow servant fell to his knees and begged him, 'Be patient with me, and I will pay you back.'
>
> "But he refused. Instead, he went off and had the man thrown into prison until he could pay the debt.

When the other servants saw what had happened, they were greatly distressed and went and told their master everything that had happened.

"Then the master called the servant in. 'You wicked servant,' he said, 'I canceled all that debt of yours because you begged me to. Shouldn't you have had mercy on your fellow servant just as I had on you?' In anger, his master turned him over to the jailers to be tortured, until he should pay back all he owed.

"This is how my heavenly Father will treat each of you unless you forgive your brother from your heart."

When we sin, we open the door for the devil and his demons (the jailers) to attack us with sickness; this is the torture to which Jesus refers.

I ran into a classic illustration of this cause-and-effect relationship when I ministered in the TAG healing room in the 1970s. A woman with rheumatoid arthritis came into the prayer room. She was in excruciating pain, and her hands were so deformed with severe knots that she couldn't open them. I prayed for her several times and nothing happened. Then I asked her a question based on a word of knowledge: "Do you have any bitterness toward anyone whom you have not forgiven?"

Without any hesitation she said, "Yes, my late husband. He died five years ago. I hated him then, and I hate him still today!"

I thought, *Man, the guy is dead, and she still hates him!*

So I asked her if she was a Christian.

"Yes, I gave my life to the Lord several years ago," was her answer.

"So, if God has forgiven you of your sins, who are you to

withhold forgiveness from another?" I asked gently. I didn't want to be mean, but I wanted to speak the truth in love.

She responded, "But you don't know what kind of man he was. He was terribly abusive, and I would feel like a hypocrite if I forgave him because I have absolutely no feelings for him."

"Ma'am," I said, "I'm sure what your husband did was horrible, and I am in no way justifying his actions. All I am asking is for you to do *yourself* a favor and forgive him, because I believe your bitterness is blocking God from healing you."

"Well, I have no feelings for him."

"Forgiveness is not based on feelings. And sooner or later you have to forgive. But five years has been too long, and it is crippling you with arthritis. I tell you what, why don't I lead you in a prayer of repentance and forgiveness, and you can just repeat after me."

With that I began to lead her in a prayer, just as I would a person who wanted to pray the sinner's prayer. She was repeating every word verbatim until we got to "and I forgive my late husband." She could barely get the words out. Finally, as she confessed, she started to sob. All the years of pent-up bitterness poured out of her heart.

What is amazing is that I didn't have to pray for her healing. As soon as she began to weep in genuine repentance, she said, "Look, I can move my fingers. The pain is gone!"

God had taken the poison of bitterness out of her body as she forgave her late husband.

The Hatred Sins

Another major root issue of sickness that can stymie God in answering prayer consists of what I call the sins of hatred. These violations include racism, unrighteous judgment and anger.[2] My conviction that such sins block healing is supported by plenty of Scriptures and plenty of examples. Here is a real-life illustration of how serious this problem is in the Body of Christ.

My first time ministering in Austria, I was speaking at a national leaders' conference and had been asked to open the gathering with a healing service. During the worship, I kept getting the strong sense that there was a spirit of anti-Semitism among the leaders of the conference. I didn't know what to do with this word! I didn't want to preach to pastors on anti-Semitism my first time in this conference, let alone the first time visiting the country—it is not the type of message that endears you to people. But I had to obey the Holy Spirit.

I gave a message on reconciliation in general, and near the end of the message I addressed the sins of anti-Semitism. When I gave the altar call for pastors and leaders who wanted to repent, I almost fell over. It seemed like everyone stood up. To say the least, we had a great healing service. One Austrian leader said that in all his years of attending healing meetings, he had never before seen such demonstrative acts of God. I believe this happened because God honored the humility of the leaders there as they repented of the sin of anti-Semitism.

I have seen others healed of heart problems and even hemorrhoids as they repented of hatred and anger. We should all ask the Lord to give us wisdom to know if our sickness is connected to these hatred sins or to any sin.

3. SINS THAT OTHERS COMMIT AGAINST US

If we commit sins against others, that means that others are certainly committing sins against us. Someone lies, cheats, has an affair, steals, commits a murder, plays politics at work—go ahead pick the offense—and it hurts someone else. Whenever this happens, it creates a spiritual environment in which Satan can operate or at the very least try to gain a foothold.

Sins that others commit against us include molestation and abuse, whether emotional, physical or sexual. When something traumatic happens to a person, a demonic spirit can attack him or her at a point of vulnerability. This spirit or the trauma of the abuse itself can break down the immune system, opening the door to all kinds of sicknesses. I have also noticed that abuse can lead to other demonic activity such as depression, eating disorders and even suicidal tendencies.

In February 2002, my wife and I were ministering at a conference in Brisbane, Australia. A young girl with severe scoliosis approached us. For over 10 years, she had also suffered from fibromyalgia (an autoimmune disorder resulting in aches and pains throughout the entire body). She came forward because she had felt pain leave her body when I gave a word of knowledge concerning fibromyalgia. She whispered in my ear that she had all sorts of other illnesses. I sensed in my heart that she had been abused and that there was a spirit of suicide over her life. I didn't want to embarrass her, so I whispered into her ear, commanding the spirit of suicide to leave. She instantly fell onto the floor and began to manifest demonic activity. I knelt down and ministered to her. Later, I found out that what I had discerned was true and that she had wanted to take her life. God healed her completely that night!

In these kinds of cases there is great opportunity for the victims to forgive, but sometimes pastors can't minister effectively to these people from the pulpit alone. More is needed. Problems such as these are often deep-rooted and require specialized help. In such cases, inner emotional healing is needed. Harvest Rock Church has a team of counselors who are trained to minister to those who have been traumatized by abuse and neglect. I also recommend the ministry of Elijah House, run by John and Paula Sanford, and the Healing House Ministry, directed by Chester and Betsy Kylstra.

4. SINS OF OUR FATHERS: GENERATIONAL SINS AND CURSES

Exodus 20:5 declares:

> You shall not bow down to them or worship them; for I, the LORD your God, am a jealous God, punishing the children for the sin of the fathers to the third and fourth generation of those who hate me.

It is clear that the sins of the fathers, as well as the judgments brought by those sins, can be passed down to the third and fourth generations. The good news is, "Christ redeemed us from the curse of the law by becoming a curse for us, for it is written: 'Cursed is everyone who is hung on a tree' " (Gal. 3:13).

I am not a doctor. I am a pastor. But from a spiritual perspective, I believe that any generational sickness may be due to a genetic defect resulting from the sins of one generation being passed on to the next generation.

I have observed that sicknesses, such as allergies, asthma, heart disease, diabetes and depression, often seem to be passed down from one member of the family to the next generation. I have seen each of these types of sicknesses healed when the generational sickness has been broken.

When C. Peter Wagner was still a professor at Fuller Theological Seminary and I was taking one of my doctorate classes from him, there was a student present in class who was suffering from allergies. Peter knew I operated in the gift of healing, so he asked me to pray for him. Instead of praying a general prayer, I prayed a prayer of authority, breaking the generational curse of allergies and commanding the spirit of allergies to leave him. He was healed instantly, right there in class.[3]

5. SINS THAT WE COMMIT AGAINST OURSELVES

Now we come to what I call the mother of all sins—those we commit against ourselves.

Jesus said, "Love your neighbor as yourself" (Matt. 22:39). God assumes that we love and accept ourselves; He commands us to love and accept others in a similar manner. But I find so many people in the Church today who hate themselves, their bodies or the way they look. They hate their fatness, their personality or their level of intelligence. As a result, they constantly curse themselves. These are the sins of self-hatred, self-rejection, low self-esteem, guilt and condemnation.

God has given us a wonderful immune system. As a non-medical person, my understanding is that white cells were created to fight sickness. But when these cells go awry and attack our own body, it can lead to a variety of illnesses. For example:

1. In some forms of arthritis, the white cells attack the joints.
2. Unrestricted growth of white blood cells can lead to several different forms of cancer.
3. A variety of autoimmune disorders, such as fibromyalgia rheumatica and lupus, result from white blood cells attacking other systems in the body.

In a similar manner, when we attack ourselves with self-hatred or any other sin against ourselves, we can become physically ill.

I have observed that some of the most dramatic healings take place when people repent of self-hatred. A classic example is the healing Jan-Aage Torp, a pastor and friend of mine from Norway, experienced. Jan-Aage had severe diabetes. He was sleeping 12 to 14 hours a day. He was also going blind. He came to a conference in Singapore at which I was speaking. I gave a lesson on how diabetes can often be rooted in self-rejection and self-hatred. Something hit home with him. He came to the altar to repent of self-rejection. I prayed for him. He didn't feel any different at that moment, but he went back to his hotel room to test his blood sugar level. To his amazement his blood sugar level had improved by 50 percent! Later he e-mailed me and informed me that he had lost 105 pounds, that his weight was now stable and that his eyesight had been restored. The doctors were amazed that he no longer had diabetes. To say the least, God performed a miracle; and now Jan-Aage is a member of Harvest International Ministries, our apostolic network.

Sexual sins also fall into this category. When a person commits a sexual sin, he or she is sinning against him- or herself. That is what the Bible records in 1 Corinthians 6:18: "Flee from sexual immorality. All other sins a man commits are outside his body, but he who sins sexually sins against his own body."

Of all the sins that have devastated world health, the primary ones have been sexual in nature. What God gave as a beautiful gift to be shared in the context of marriage, people have perverted. As a result, we have a pandemic problem of sexually transmitted diseases.

- The number of sexually transmitted diseases has rapidly grown over the past two decades.
- Every nine months a new sexually transmitted disease is discovered.
- Twelve million people contract a sexually transmitted disease every year in America alone. That is 33,000 a day.
- In 1996, 5 of the top 10 reported infectious diseases (including the top 4) were sexually transmitted.[4]

> # SOME OF THE MOST DRAMATIC HEALINGS TAKE PLACE WHEN PEOPLE REPENT OF SELF-HATRED.

These statistics do not even begin to address the AIDS virus, which is decimating the African population.

Finally, I want to briefly share about a sin that most pastors don't preach on and that requires a great deal of sensitivity—the sin of gluttony. The Bible teaches that the human body is the temple of the Holy Spirit. In 1 Corinthians 3:16-17, we learn, "Don't you know that you yourselves are God's temple and that God's Spirit lives in you? If anyone destroys God's temple, God will destroy him; for God's temple is sacred, and you are that temple." God's Word further declares, "So whether you eat or drink or whatever you do, do it all for the glory of God" (1 Cor. 10:31). Unfortunately, many of us in the Body of Christ do not take this seriously; instead, we abuse our bodies by eating too much sugar and too many refined carbohydrates and fatty foods, which simply are not good for us. As a result, many of us are suffering from diseases ranging from diabetes to heart disease, not to mention obesity, which leads to chronic backaches and pain throughout the body. The human body was never intended to carry that much weight. To eat such unhealthy foods—and so much of it— is a sin against our bodies.

I also believe that we are testing God by asking Him to heal our diseases and pains that are the result of poor eating habits and lack of exercise, when we are not willing to change these habits. Please forgive me. I do not want to sound condemning in any way. As I said earlier, this is a sensitive area, but my heart aches for people who come to me for healing when the fundamental issue is something that they can change by God's grace.

I am a pastor, not a nutritionist, but here is what I recommend:

1. Receive inner healing and deliverance if there are root emotional and spiritual issues underlying the poor eating habits.
2. Stay away from sugar and refined carbohydrates. Read *The South Beach Diet, Sugar Busters!* or a similar book.[5]
3. Avoid fatty meats and fatty foods. I believe in a high-protein diet, but I personally believe that we need to be careful here. Today most of the meats we eat have so many added hormones that there is concern these hormones may be the cause for some types of cancer, such as breast cancer. Instead, eat lean protein like turkey, chicken and fish.
4. Exercise, exercise, exercise. I believe that everyone needs to do at least 20 to 30 minutes of aerobic

exercise three times a week, as a minimum.

5. Read about and study the subject of proper nutrition. Carole Lewis, Don Colbert and Pamela Smith have written wonderful books about healthy living from a biblical perspective.[6]

A NOTE ABOUT DOCTORS

What do I do when I get a headache? I pray first, but I will also use aspirin. What would I do if a relative had cancer? I would pray for healing first, but I would also recommend that he or she visit the finest medical professionals in the world. God heals—there is no doubt. He also works through doctors, nurses, emergency medical technicians and other medical professionals.

Should someone stop taking medicine in hopes of being healed? C. Peter Wagner wrote:

A medical doctor is the only one who has the authority to remove a patient from a prescribed medication. Those who believe they have received healing for a condition requiring medication should check with their doctor before altering their prescribed treatment.[7]

Most people in healing ministries agree that God works through medicine as well as through miracles. Francis MacNutt gives us a good perspective:

Ordinarily, of course, God works through doctors, psychiatrists, counselors and nurses to facilitate nature's healing process. This may seem so obvious as to go without saying, except that there are some Christians who set up an artificial opposition between prayer and medicine—as if God's way of healing is through prayer, while the medical profession is a secular means of healing somehow unworthy of Christians who have real faith. Consequently, they encourage people to pray and not to see their doctor. But God works through the doctor to heal as well as through prayer for healing—the doctor, the counselor and the nurse are all ministers of healing. . . .

We need to learn to work as a team, rather than as competitors, to bring God's healing power to the entire Christian body.[8]

To get an idea of the team MacNutt talks about, reread the story about Ryan Corbin in chapter 5. The UCLA trauma unit saved Ryan's life, but the continuing process of his healing would not be happening if it were not for the faith team and millions of prayers.

TAKE A PERSONAL INVENTORY

Although I haven't done justice to the very important subject of how we sabotage our own health through sin, including our attitudes, actions and habits, I felt that I would be less than honest if I had not at least touched on this area. If this list of sins speaks to your heart, I want to lead you in a prayer at the end of the next chapter. It is a prayer of repentance and renunciation of sin, as well as a prayer for deliverance from any demonic spirits that may be behind your sin and sickness. The prayer ends with a declaration of faith for your healing—pray it and believe God for it!

Notes

1. F. F. Bosworth, *Christ the Healer* (Grand Rapids, MI: Fleming H. Revell, 2000), p. 145.

2. While Jesus can forgive all of our sins, there is such a thing as righteous judgment, which is for leaders to do carefully under biblical guidelines. In other words, we should not withhold righteous judgment when it is required.

3. For more information on generational bondages and instruction on how to break them, read Cindy Jacobs, *Deliver Us from Evil* (Ventura, CA: Regal Books, 2001), pp. 225-230.

4. Winkie Pratney, speaking at Harvest Rock Church, 1999.

5. Arthur Agatston, *The South Beach Diet* (Emmaus, PA: Rodale Press, 2003); H. Leighton Steward, Morrison C. Bethea, Sam S. Andrews, et al. *Sugar Busters!* (New York: Ballantine Books, 1998).

6. Carole Lewis has produced the First Place series of books (Ventura, CA: Regal Books). Don Colbert and Pamela Smith have each published a number of books with Charisma House (formerly Creation House) of Lake Mary, Florida. These books are available at many Christian bookstores.

7. C. Peter Wagner, *How to Have a Healing Ministry* (Ventura, CA: Regal Books, 1988), p. 267.

8. Francis MacNutt, *Healing* (Notre Dame, IN: Ave Maria Press, 1974), pp. 131-132.

THE PRAYER FACTOR

God wants to heal the sick today. It is God's nature to heal
people, and he has called us to reflect his nature.

JOHN WIMBER, *POWER HEALING*

Before we pray the prayer of faith for physical healing, it is
important that we have had an opportunity to do some self-
examination to find possible root issues that can hinder healing. If the root issue is not dealt with, it will be the same as if
we chop off the top of a dandelion flower but do not pull out
the root of the weed. So that we can do this systematically, I
have outlined what I call the seven Rs of deliverance and healing. Please read them. Then I will put the seven Rs together
into one prayer of healing and deliverance.

SEVEN RS OF DELIVERANCE AND HEALING

As you pray for healing, it is helpful to follow the following seven steps.

1. Recognize the Sin

Honestly evaluate the root sins in your life. It is crucial that you honestly ask if sin is the root issue for your sickness. If this is indeed the case, the question becomes, What type of sin is it? Is it sin against God? Sins others have committed against you? The sins of your ancestors? Or sins you have committed against yourself? In order to address the root issue, it is important to repent of the sin specifically. You may want to pray what the psalmist prayed in Psalm 139:23-24:

> Search me, O God, and know my heart; test me and know my anxious thoughts. See if there is any offensive way in me, and lead me in the way everlasting.

2. Take Responsibility

Once the sins have been identified, it is important not to rationalize, shift blame or excuse your sins. Even if a sin is one committed against you, it is important to ask yourself if you harbor any bitterness or judgment toward the person who has sinned against you. If so, you need to repent of that. The difference between a mature person and an immature person is the acceptance of responsibility. A person can be mature at 17 years old by accepting the responsibility of his or her sins, or a person can be immature at 72 years old by not accepting responsibility for his or her sins. Now is the time to take responsibility for your life.

3. Reconcile

In the process of repenting of your own sin, it is important to also forgive those who have sinned against you (remember the Lord's Prayer?). I know many of you have already gone through the process of forgiveness, but let me add two more thoughts. The Bible is clear about the importance of being reconciled with others. Matthew 5:23-24 quotes Jesus:

> Therefore, if you are offering your gift at the altar and there remember that your brother has something against you, leave your gift there in front of the altar. First go and be reconciled to your brother; then come and offer your gift.

I know that some of this information will take time to process, understand and act upon, but I believe we honor God when we make a sincere effort to be reconciled. If you have sincerely tried but haven't progressed, remember the Bible clearly states that God is looking for your effort and your desire for reconciliation.

Romans 12:17-19 declares:

> Do not repay anyone evil for evil. Be careful to do what is right in the eyes of everybody. If it is possible, as far as it depends on you, live at peace with everyone. Do not take revenge, my friends, but leave room for God's wrath, for it is written: "It is mine to avenge; I will repay," says the Lord.

To be truly reconciled to another person, you must repent of any judgment made toward him or her. You can forgive someone and yet still be judging that person. To judge a person who has hurt you is to cast a decision of blame or responsibility upon him or her. Let God do the judging. Besides, you do not want to reap any judgment on your own life. "Do not judge, or you too will be judged. For in the same way you judge others, you will be judged, and with the measure you use, it will be measured to you" (Matt. 7:1-2).

4. Repent

For healing and deliverance to occur, there must be a sincere, godly sorrow for the sins that you have committed. Yes, the sins may have hurt you physically, but you have to acknowledge that your sins have first and foremost offended God. It is important that you recognize the destructiveness of sin. Sin cannot be confessed simply with your lips but must be forsaken by faith as well. In other words, recognize the sin and then stop doing it. Stop hating yourself or being bitter toward someone. This is also a great opportunity to repent of any unbelief against God.

5. Renounce

You have to take authority over any spirits that may have entered your life because of the sin or sickness. I have learned that a particular sickness may have been caused by something environmental and have nothing to do with demonic attacks. But I also know that demons love to prey on the vulnerable. Therefore, even if the cancer was caused by a dietary deficiency or by an unknown culprit, a demonic spirit may have entered. The purpose of this book is not to give a teaching on deliverance—others have done that. But I do want to stress that you have authority in Christ Jesus and that you are to use that authority to command every evil spirit to depart from your life.

6. Receive

You have to exercise faith in God's faithfulness and in His Word. It is important to lay hands on yourself according to Mark 16:17-18: "And these signs will accompany those who believe: In my name they will drive out demons; . . . they will place their hands on sick people, and they will get well."

IT IS CRUCIAL THAT AFTER YOU PRAY, YOU CONTINUE TO THANK GOD FOR YOUR HEALING, REGARDLESS OF THE MANIFESTATION.

God wants to use you to heal yourself. You have the anointing and the authority, according to God's Word. Receive your healing by faith. It is crucial that after you pray, you continue to thank God for your healing, regardless of the manifestation. As with my healing from TMJ, it may take time before the healing manifestation occurs. Or it might be a progressive healing. As I am writing this, a partially deaf woman who has been attending our church is progressively improving, no doubt because she continues to stand on the promises of God. She believes He will completely restore her hearing, in His time.

7. Renew

Finally, you need to pray that God will fill you with His Spirit, especially if any demonic spirits were cast out in step 5. Jesus said in Luke 11:24-26:

When an evil spirit comes out of a man, it goes through arid places seeking rest and does not find it. Then it says, "I will return to the house I left." When it arrives, it finds the house swept clean and put in order. Then it goes and takes seven other spirits more wicked than itself, and they go in and live there. And the final condition of that man is worse than the first.

Those in the deliverance ministry recognize the importance of praying for the patient to be filled with the Holy Spirit so that the problem won't worsen.

PRAY THIS PRAYER OF FAITH AND DELIVERANCE FOR YOUR HEALING

Place your hands over your body, targeting the specific area affected by pain or sickness. If your whole body is affected, place your hand over your head. Then, pray this prayer out loud and in faith:

Father, I come to You in Jesus' name. I ask that Your kingdom will come and Your will be done. I invoke the presence of the Holy Spirit over my life. Father, I want to repent and renounce all sin in my life [take time here to be specific and confess your sins to the Lord]. *I also forgive all those who have hurt me* [again be specific and forgive people by name]. *I repent of any judgments I have made of them. In Jesus' name I command every evil spirit that has been oppressing me to leave. I thank You that the Word of God is true. Your Word says that Jesus went about doing good, healing all who were oppressed of the devil. And it says that You are the same yesterday, today and forever. In Jesus'*

name I take authority over every spirit of sickness. I break
every generational curse of sickness over my life and the lives
of my family members. I place my hand on my body; Your
Word says I will recover. By faith I receive my healing in
Jesus' name. I receive a fresh infilling of Your Holy Spirit.
Thank You for healing me. In Jesus' name, amen.

POSTPRAYER INSTRUCTIONS

1. Continue to praise God and thank Him for the healing, whether you have received the manifestation or not. Give Him all the praise and glory for your healing. Praise and thanksgiving are the languages of faith.

2. Act on God's Word and do something physical that you couldn't do before. Remember, faith without corresponding actions is dead (see Jas. 2:17).

3. Continue to fight the good fight of faith. I have seen sickness return when people began to doubt their healing. Obviously, you want to continue in faith, regardless of whether you have received a manifestation or not.

4. If you have not received a manifestation of healing, get others to pray for you, especially your pastor (see Jas. 5:14) and those with the gifts of healing (see 1 Cor. 12:9).

5. If you have received a manifestation of your healing, go to a physician and get medical confirmation.

6. Go and sin no more (if this is relevant).

7. Finally, write to me and let me know what happened. I love to collect testimonies, so let me know! Contact me at harvestrockchurch.org.

THE GIVING FACTOR

I believe that we are on the verge of the greatest healing revival since the days of the Early Church. What makes this revival so extraordinary is that we are going to see ordinary believers move in the supernatural. That means you!

Most people in the Church are not pastors or healing evangelists, yet there are six billion people to reach on this planet. God wants to activate every born-again believer to move in signs and wonders to get the job of fulfilling the Great Commission done. Remember what I wrote in the first chapter about the most important healing of all? Again, it is not physical healing; it is the healing of our relationship with God.

As I write this, it is Sunday evening. This morning one of my church members shared a testimony of how God used her to pray for someone dying of leukemia, and after lengthy intercession the person was totally healed.

In June 2003, Harvest International Ministries (HIM) sponsored a retreat on the East Coast of the United States. HIM apostolic team members Charles and Ann Stock hosted the gathering. After the retreat, the Stocks asked me if I would conduct a healing service at their church. I asked Charles if there was anyone who had had a remarkable healing and would be willing to testify before I taught and prayed for the sick. He told me about a man who had been healed of a cancerous tumor in his throat. That night the man gave his testimony, explaining how he had been diagnosed with a tumor in his throat and that he had gone to the Healing Room in Lancaster, Pennsylvania. There, a layperson who had been trained to pray for the sick through the Healing Room Ministries prayed for him. Soon after receiving this prayer, the man with the tumor was driving his work truck when he started to cough up blood. He pulled the truck over to the side of the road, and the condition worsened. It dawned on him that maybe he should save some of the blood that he was coughing up for the doctors to examine. He emptied the coffee out of his thermos and began to cough up more blood. As he was coughing, a large tumor the size of his hand came out of his throat and fell into the mug. He was instantly healed of his throat cancer.

Both testimonies are examples of how God is using ordinary believers to pray for extraordinary healings. There are many Scriptures that support the idea that God uses every Christian to do the works of Jesus. Here are a few of them:

- Mark 16:15-18—"He said to them, 'Go into all the world and preach the good news to all creation. Whoever believes and is baptized will be saved, but whoever does not believe will be condemned. *And these signs will accompany those who believe:* In my name they will drive out demons; they will speak in new tongues; they will pick up snakes with their hands; and when they drink deadly poison, it will not hurt them at all; *they will place their hands on sick people, and they will get well'* "(emphasis added). Laying hands on the sick is not just for pastors or healing evangelists for that matter (see Jas. 5:14-16). The Bible clearly states that these signs will follow those who believe in Jesus.

- John 14:12-14—"I tell you the truth, *anyone who has faith in me* will do what I have been doing. He *will do even greater things than these*, because I am going to the Father. And I will do whatever you ask in my name, so that the Son may bring glory to the Father. You may ask me for anything in my name, and I will do it" (emphasis added).

· Acts 2:17-19—"In the last days, God says, I will pour out my Spirit on all people. Your sons and daughters will prophesy, your young men will see visions, your old men will dream dreams. Even on my servants, both men and women, I will pour out my Spirit in those days, and they will prophesy. I will show wonders in the heaven above and signs on the earth below." I believe that all those who receive God's Spirit will be able to exercise spiritual gifts like prophecy, but God also wants to use His people to do signs of healing on the earth.

· Ephesians 4:11-13 (*NKJV*)—"And He Himself gave some to be apostles, some prophets, some evangelists, and some pastors and teachers, for the equipping of the saints for the work of ministry, for the edifying of the body of Christ, till we all come to the unity of the faith and of the knowledge of the Son of God, to a perfect man, to the measure of the stature of the fullness of Christ." This Scripture is the most exciting for me. I believe that God has given to the Church apostles, prophets, evangelists, pastors and teachers to *equip the saints* for the work of ministry. I believe what Bishop Bill Hamon and other leaders are saying: We are in the day of the saints. It is now time for the saints (that means you—the Bible refers to all believers in Jesus as saints) to do the work of praying for the sick.

I wrote the preceding chapters to help you receive a healing by applying the basic principles of healing to your own life. In this final section I want to equip you with practical steps on how you can pray for others who are sick. I want to teach you in an inductive way, posing questions that you may have and answer them in a way that will teach you how to effectively pray for the sick.

WHAT IF I DO NOT HAVE THE GIFT OF HEALING?

That is a good question. The Bible explains the gifts of healing in 1 Corinthians 12:7-11:

> Now to each one the manifestation of the Spirit is given for the common good. To one there is given through the Spirit the message of wisdom, to another the message of knowledge by means of the same Spirit, to another faith by the same Spirit, to another gifts of healing by that one Spirit, to another miraculous powers, to another prophecy, to another distinguishing between spirits, to another speaking in different kinds of tongues, and to still another the interpretation of tongues. All these are the work of one and the same Spirit, and he gives them to each one, just as he determines.

We must understand the difference between a gift and a role. Not everyone has the gift of evangelism (see Eph. 4:11), but every believer's role is to share the good news of our Lord Jesus Christ. Not everyone has the gift of giving either.

Romans 12:6-8 explains:

> We have different gifts, according to the grace given us.
> If a man's gift is prophesying, let him use it in propor-
> tion to his faith. If it is serving, let him serve; if it is teach-
> ing, let him teach; if it is encouraging, let him encourage;
> if it is contributing to the needs of others, let him give
> generously; if it is leadership, let him govern diligently; if
> it is showing mercy, let him do it cheerfully.

We are all to give of our resources to advance God's kingdom.
That is the role of a good and responsible follower of Jesus. In
the passage just cited, the Bible refers to the gift of serving. I
don't particularly have that gift, but I also know that the Bible
teaches that I am to serve others in love (see Gal. 5:13).
Therefore, even though we may not have the gift of healing,
the Word of God clearly states that as believers we are to pray
for the sick and they will recover (see Mark 16:18).

WHERE AND WHEN SHOULD
I PRAY FOR THE SICK?

Praying for the sick should be something that is a natural part
of your life as a believer. I call it living the supernatural natural life. If someone is sick and asks for prayer, you should pray
for that person right then and there.

How about praying for those who do not specifically ask for
prayer? You can begin with your family members. When a family or close relative is sick, ask if you can pray for him or her. I have
rarely had anyone, including unbelievers, reject prayer when he
or she is sick. You can also pray for people who are in your church
or who are part of your circle of fellowship. This may include

friends or members of a small group. Finally, take the initiative to pray for strangers when the Holy Spirit leads you to do so. You do not have to go up to every person who is sick and ask if he or she wants prayer, but do not hesitate to pray for someone who is sick or to approach the person if God prompts you to act.

I remember a time when I was flying on an airplane, and as soon as the seat-belt sign went off, a man sitting in front of me jumped up and just stood next to the restroom. When the flight attendant approached him and asked if anything was wrong, he told her that he had pinched a nerve in his back and couldn't sit without excruciating pain. I was in hearing distance of the conversation, and I felt led by the Holy Spirit to approach him. I told him that I believed in the power of prayer and asked if I could pray for him. His reply was that he could use all the help he could get. Once I had the man's permission to pray, I placed my hand on his back and rebuked the pain in Jesus' name; he was instantly healed. He didn't accept Jesus Christ at that moment, but the impact of God's touch was profound.

HOW SHOULD WE PRAY FOR THE SICK?

There are many ways to pray for the sick. Here is a five-step process that I learned from the late John Wimber when I took his and Peter Wagner's course on signs and wonders and church growth at Fuller Theological Seminary in the fall of 1984. Even though that was many years ago, these steps are time tested. I know because I still use them today. I have paraphrased the following from Wimber by using the first person to show how we can all follow these steps:

1. Interview: Where does it hurt? I ask the person who is sick simply what is wrong with him or her. Now,

I am not a doctor, so I am not after any medical detail; I simply want to know what the problem is and where it hurts. The person I am praying for may tell me about something simple, "I have a splitting headache," or about something major, "I have just returned from the doctor and he says that I have breast cancer."

2. Diagnostic Decision: What is causing this condition? This is where I have to ask Jesus to give me discernment about whether the problem is caused by sin (see chapter 7) or the demonic or whether it is simply a physiological problem. Usually the rule of thumb I follow is that if the pain is recent due to an accident, it is usually a physiological problem. People do have accidents. When a problem is chronic, or long term, and the doctors don't know why the problem persists, that is when I begin to ask the Holy Spirit if it is rooted in the demonic. If it is rooted in sin, I tactfully ask whether or not there was any sin that may have opened the door for the sickness.

3. Prayer Selection: What kind of prayer should I use? I have several different types of prayer that I can choose. Intercessory prayer is simply asking God to heal the person. It may go something like "Heavenly Father, I come to You in Jesus' name. I ask that You would heal my friend of the [name the sickness] in Jesus' name. Amen." Command prayer is a type of prayer that Jesus used on many occasions. In fact, the type of prayer that Jesus used most often was command prayer, to command healing or to command sickness or demons to

leave (for examples just in the Gospel of Mark, see Mark 1:21-26,40-42; 2:11-12; 3:1-5; 5:41-42). Rebuke prayer is like command prayer, but it applies when I know that the root issue is demonic. If it is demonic, I can pray something like "In Jesus' name, I bind this spirit of cancer and I command that this spirit come out immediately!"

4. Prayer Engagement: How are we doing? When I am praying, I pray with my eyes open so that I can see what the Holy Spirit is doing. Then I select one of the prayers mentioned above and engage in prayer. After prayer I ask the person how he or she feels. It is very important that I get the person to be honest about his or her symptoms. If the person does not sense anything different, he or she needs to say that so that I can continue to pray. Then I ask the Lord how long and how often I should pray for the person. This is where I have to be led by the Holy Spirit once again. There have been times when I have prayed for the sick and nothing happens, but the Holy Spirit clearly instructs me to keep soaking the person with intercessory prayer. Then the person starts to gradually get better. When the Holy Spirit tells me to stop, I stop.[1]

5. Postprayer Direction: What should I do now? This is where I can tell the person to continue to thank God for the healing, whether or not he or she has received a manifestation of the healing. Or I can encourage the person to continue to confess God's promises concerning healing from the Bible (see appendix B). I also tell the person that if he or she has received a manifestation of healing, to get a

doctor's verification. Most people will receive a partial healing, and I encourage them to fight the good fight of faith and continue to confess the words found in Mark 11:22-24: " 'Have faith in God,' Jesus answered. 'I tell you the truth, if anyone says to this mountain, "Go, throw yourself into the sea," and does not doubt in his heart but believes that what he says will happen, it will be done for him. Therefore I tell you, whatever you ask for in prayer, believe that you have received it, and it will be yours.' " But I make it into a confession of faith and tell them to continually confess something like "I believe that I have received a healing by faith."[2]

Let me close with the words that Jesus spoke to the seventy-two disciples. These were not the apostles, but I believe the seventy-two represent people such as you and me. Look at Luke 10:1-2,8-9:

After this the Lord appointed seventy-two others and sent them two by two ahead of him to every town and place where he was about to go. He told them, "The harvest is plentiful, but the workers are few. Ask the Lord of the harvest, therefore, to send out workers into his harvest field. When you enter a town and are welcomed, eat what is set before you. Heal the sick who are there and tell them, 'The kingdom of God is near you.' "

Jesus says to you, "Heal the sick and cast out demons. Freely you have received, now freely give!" (see Matt. 10:8).

Notes

1. For more information about hearing God's voice, read Cindy Jacobs, *The Voice of God* (Ventura, CA: Regal Books, 1995); Chuck D. Pierce and Rebecca Wagner Sytsema, *When God Speaks* (Colorado Springs, CO: Wagner Publications, 2003); and Jack Deere, *Surprised by the Voice of God* (Grand Rapids, MI: Zondervan Publishing House, 1998).
2. John Wimber, course MC510 "Signs, Wonders and Church Growth," Fuller Theological Seminary, 1984; for additional information, see John Wimber with Kevin Springer, *Power Healing* (San Francisco: Harper and Row, 1987), pp. 198-210.

The Mystery of God's Healing Power

Pat Robertson and His 700 Club Cohosts
Answer Questions About Sickness, Prayer and
God's Desire to Restore

Question: How do you get divine healing? I've been
praying for healing for my mom, who suffers from
congestive heart failure and bad lungs.

Pat (Robertson): I remember Kathryn Kuhlman saying
that every time she thought she had God figured
out, He changed the way He did things. He is infinite and all-powerful. Jesus went about doing
good and healing all who were oppressed of the
devil and all who were sick. Everyone who came
to Him for healing got healed. I don't know of
anybody He turned down, so it is God's plan
and will to heal people—physically as well as
spiritually.

How do you get it? You have to empty yourself
and ask Him. Sometimes it is spontaneous. I
believe it was in Toronto that a fellow was walking
along the street. There were TV sets in a window of
an appliance store and he stood outside. There was
a word of knowledge that came during a telethon.
He received it and was healed. He didn't know the
Lord, but all of a sudden—bingo!—God describes
him and God heals him.

Don't ask me why the Lord does what He does when He does it. Normally speaking, when we pray and we seek His face and we ask Him, He will do something. He says, "When you stand praying, if you have ought against any, forgive that your Heavenly Father might forgive you" [Mark 11:25]. It is very important that we do forgive others, because it depends on entering into the supernatural with the Lord.

Terry (Meeuwsen): Also, Pat, I will hear people say, "I was praying, 'God, please let them say something for me.'" You don't have to have a word of knowledge specifically about your condition to be healed, do you?

Pat: Of course you don't, but some people like to do that. I think it was Harold Bredesen, our good friend and brother for many years, who was praying in a church. These people were coming in a prayer line and he was laying hands on people and the Lord was showing him what was going on. This one woman came up for prayer and he laid hands on her. He said, "I don't think there is anything wrong with you." She said, "I don't think so, either. I just came for a checkup."

It isn't like a magic trick where you ask, "Could you give a word of knowledge for me?" The biggest thing is that the word is in the Bible. It is in Isaiah 53 and all throughout the New Testament and in all of the Gospels about the healing power of God.

Question: I know that healing is promised in the Word of God as part of the New Covenant, but why do we see so little healing and miracles in our churches today?

Pat: Do you remember what Jesus said to the church in Laodicea? "You are rich. You are increased with goods, having need of nothing." I think that describes American Christianity. We are rich and increased with goods and have need of nothing.

Jesus said, "Blessed are the spiritual beggars, for theirs is the kingdom of God" [Matthew 5:3]. You have to be really desperate. When you get desperate with God, things start happening. Why should you want healing if you can go to see the doctor? If you have a headache, he will give you an aspirin. If you are a little emotional, he gives you Prozac. If you have something wrong with your skin, he scrapes it off. If your hip doesn't work, he gives you a new one. We have gotten used to doctors and medicine that take care of these things. We are not desperate. But when we begin to get desperate with God, we begin to see miracles.

Question: In the Bible it states that by His stripes we are healed. Then why do some people still die of disease?

Pat: I don't think it means that every person in the world is healed by the stripes of Jesus, but He bore, potentially on His body, the sicknesses and diseases of everybody. Not everybody gets forgiven of their sins. He took our sins on Himself when He was nailed to the cross, but everybody is not forgiven of sins. I do think we have to ask. We have to obtain it.

Is that the question: why doesn't everybody get healed?

Gordon (Robertson): Right. Why do some people still die of disease?

Pat: That is Universalism, like the [belief that the] salvation of Jesus is for everybody. It is potentially, but you still have to accept Him as Savior. For healing, you have to accept the stripes for you.

Question: I want to see a miracle of healing for a friend who has had cancer for five years. I know the answer could be "no," but how do I know that I'm praying correctly and will see results?

Pat: I wish I could tell you. I stood over the corpse of a dead girl who had been embalmed in a church and asked the Lord to raise her up. It didn't happen, because the Lord had already told me, "Blessed are they that die in the Lord from henceforth." God was taking that child home.

On the other hand, I prayed for somebody else, and I wanted to wait and make sure they were dead before I got there because I didn't want to interfere with God. He was dying, so I waited and eventually got to the hospital. The guy was still alive, so two of us down in Colombia prayed for him, and in the name of Jesus, spoke. They told us when we went in, "You may get him up, but he will be a vegetable." God raised him out of a coma, lifted him up, and he's the only bilingual vegetable I ever saw! The Lord touched him. It was a miracle.

I saw one woman who the Lord healed. She wanted to stay alive a few more years to raise her children. The doctors said she was going to die, but she didn't die.

Terry: There is a sovereignty issue involved in this,

certainly. We ask because God tells us to ask, but we have to always understand that His purposes are different from ours and higher from ours [see Isaiah 55:8].

Pat: You have to be sensitive to the Lord and ask Him. God will show you what He's going to do. The faith is the faith of God, and He will give the word. When you are there praying for somebody, He will give faith in your heart that this is going to happen. He will speak to you. Sometimes He will say no, it is not going to happen. That is a question of being sensitive to Him. Many times we see through a glass darkly. We know in part and we prophesy in part [see 1 Corinthians 13: 9]. For anyone to say he has a clear channel and he knows everything is coming from God, I don't think I have met anybody like that yet.

Gordon: I think the issue may be praying correctly. How do I know I am praying correctly? We want to get into the form, so that if we execute the ritual in the proper method and the proper time and quote the proper Scripture, it is almost like it is a magic formula. We are getting away from truly relying on God. Jesus said I see the Father work and I work [see John 5:19], and that makes it really easy. You look to Jesus, the Author and Finisher of our faith, and He speaks words. And you just say, "OK, I will bring myself in line with that."

Pat: The way that power is transmitted is the mind of God to the Spirit of God to the spirit of man to the mind of man and to the mouth of man. You look to the Father and listen to what He is saying. He speaks to your spirit, and your spirit speaks to your mind, and then you command the disease to go, you command the cancer to leave, you command the demon to come out, and you command the person who is paralyzed to stand up and walk. That's what you read over and over again: "In the name of Jesus, rise and walk."

Gordon: One of the best prayers in the Bible is the centurion's prayer: "Lord, speak the word and my servant will be healed" [see Matthew 8:5-13].[1]

Note

1. Pat Robertson, "The Mystery of God's Healing Power," *CBN.com*, 2003. http://cbn.org/700club/askpat/BIO_divinehealing.asp (accessed September 11, 2003). Reprinted with permission.

BIBLICAL DECLARATIONS TO BUILD STRONG FAITH

Larry Tomczak

Those who seek the LORD lack no good thing.
PSALM 34:10

You are the only being in the universe that can cause defeat in your life. Wholeheartedly *decide,* by the grace of God and the power of His Holy Spirit, to please God; and all the demons in hell, all the people in the world, all your apparent weaknesses, shortcomings, inadequacies, adverse circumstances and unfavorable surroundings *cannot* prevent you from having glorious victory! You can do all things through Christ who strengthens you!

The key to this decision is to totally surrender to Jesus as Lord and then discover by revelation and meditation who you are in Christ. "If anyone is *in Christ,* he is a new creation; old things have passed away; behold, all things have become new" (2 Cor. 5:17, *NKJV,* emphasis added).

We are not to live defeated lives, bound up in fear, doubt, unbelief; deceived into thinking we are still in bondage to sin, Satan and feelings. God's intention is that we live victoriously. We are to "live by faith." We are free from sin and condemnation, guilt and fear. We are a "new creation." Jesus said, "I came that you might have life and have it in abundance" (see John

10:10). See yourself as God sees you. Step out of your ability and step into God's ability, and you will live a victorious Christian life.

We are not to contend with Satan for a place in victory; we are to overcome him from our position of victory. You can live in resurrection power. As a Christian, you don't have to be vexed by any compulsive habit. It is one thing to know you are forgiven of your sins; it's another thing to realize you are totally freed from sin's power! Every provision has been made for you to live victoriously. God never commands us to do something He doesn't fully equip us to do. Stop this defeatist mentality, failure consciousness, sin consciousness; it is not a matter of *do*. It is *done*! You are not just an old sinner, saved by grace. You were; but now by grace you are no longer a sinner—you are a "new creation." And it is no longer a matter of *can* or can't. It's *will* or won't. Every provision has been made for you to live victoriously.

Don't let ignorance or indolence rob you of the abundant life freely available to you. "Man does not live on bread alone, but on every word that comes from the mouth of God" (Matt. 4:4). The time to get into spiritual shape is *now*! The time to develop and then release your faith is *now*. The greatest tests in life come unannounced. Therefore, we must prepare now. The wind and rain and storms come to everyone. You must pay the price. There are no shortcuts. Commit yourself to daily spend time in His presence developing your love relationship with Him and cultivating a sensitivity to His voice. Also, you've been given a measure of faith and you need to develop it now.

Commit yourself to daily reading the following verses from the Word of God at the start of your day. Read them aloud. "Faith comes by *hearing*, and hearing by the word of God" (Rom. 10:17, *NKJV*, emphasis added). Read them with conviction. "Serve wholeheartedly, as if you were serving the Lord, not men" (Eph. 6:7). Husbands and wives can read them together. On the authority of the Word of God, I promise you success if you will take God's Word seriously and pay the price. Jesus is the "Apostle and High Priest of our confession" (Heb. 3:1, *NKJV*)—"Can two walk together, unless they are agreed?" (Amos 3:3, *NKJV*). We must train to say the same thing as God says in His Word. Therefore begin to meditate upon your glorious God and His loving and active Word.

"This book of the law shall not depart from your mouth, but you shall meditate on it day and night, so that you may be careful to do according to all that is written in it; for then you will make your way prosperous, and then you will have success" (Josh. 1:8, *NASB*).

"The word is near you, in your mouth and in your heart" (Rom. 10:8, *NKJV*).

WHO WE ARE IN CHRIST

As [a man] thinks in his heart, so is he.
PROVERBS 23:7, *NKJV*

Just say the word.
MATTHEW 8:8

Apart from Jesus Christ, I can do nothing; but in Jesus Christ I can do all things, so I can bring glory to Him. Therefore, I see myself as He sees me according to His living Word, for my life is "hid with Christ in God." I will train myself to say the same things as God says in His Word, for "can two walk together, unless they are agreed?"

Through regular time in His presence, I will cultivate a sensitivity to hearing His voice. He will make His Word a reality in my life as I nurture my friendship with Him. Faith will not be a formula or technique in my life but the natural by-product of knowing Him intimately as *my* faithful Lord. Knowing Him, I can totally trust Him. His Word will always be the final authority in my life. I base my entire life upon Him and His living Word. Because I meditate upon His Word day and night and carefully do all that is written in it, my way shall be prosperous.

I will be a success to the glory of God. All His blessings shall come upon me and overtake me because I obey the voice of the Lord, my God. Of this I am confident: Those who seek the Lord shall not lack any good thing. I will not live by bread alone but by every word (current utterance) that proceeds out of the mouth of God.

VICTORY

I'm not just an ordinary man or woman; I'm a son of the living God. I'm not just a person; I'm an heir of God and a joint-heir with Jesus Christ. I'm not just an old sinner; I'm a new creation in Jesus, my Lord. I'm part of a chosen generation, a royal priesthood, a holy nation; I'm one of God's people. I'm not under guilt or condemnation. I refuse discouragement, for it is not of God. God is the God of all encouragement. There is therefore now no condemnation for those in Christ Jesus. Satan is a liar. I will not listen to his accusations. I gird up the loins of my mind. I am cleansed in the blood. No weapon formed against me shall prosper and I shall confute every tongue rising against me in judgment. My mind is being renewed by the Word of God. I pull down strongholds; I cast down imaginations; I bring every thought captive to the obedience of Christ.

I am accepted in the beloved. If God be for me, who can be against me? Greater is He that is in me than he that is in the world. Nothing can separate me from the love of Christ. As the Father loves Jesus, so does Jesus love me. I'm the righteousness of God in Christ. I'm not a slave to sin; I'm a slave of God and a slave of righteousness. I continue in His Word; I know the truth and the truth has set me free. Because the Son sets me free, I am free indeed. He who is born of God keeps him and the evil one does not touch him. I've been delivered out of the kingdom of darkness. I'm now part of the kingdom of God. I don't have to serve sin anymore. Sin has no dominion over me.

I will not believe the enemy's lies. He will not intimidate me. He is a liar and the father of lies. Satan is defeated. For this purpose the Son of God came into the world, to destroy the works of the devil. No longer will he oppress me. Surely oppression makes a wise man mad. I will get mad at the devil. I defeat him by the blood of the Lamb, by the Word of my testimony, loving not my life unto death. I will submit to God. I will resist the devil and he will flee. No temptation will overtake me that is not common to man. God is faithful: He will not let me be tempted beyond my strength but with the temptation will also provide the way of escape that I may be able to endure.

I will stand fast in the liberty wherewith Christ has made me free. Where the Spirit of the Lord is, there is liberty. The law of the Spirit of life in Christ Jesus has set me free from the law of sin and death. Christ always causes me to triumph. I'll reign as a king in life through Christ Jesus. As a young man I am strong; the Word of God abides in me; and I have overcome the evil one. I am more than a conqueror through Christ who loves me. I am an overcomer. In the will of God, I am invincible. I can do all things *through Christ* who strengthens me. Thanks be to God who gives me the victory through Jesus Christ, my Lord!

FAITH

I can do all things through Christ who strengthens me. By my God I can run through a troop and leap over a wall! He makes my feet like hinds feet; He makes me walk upon high places. With man this is impossible, but with God all things are possible! All things are possible to him that believes. If I have faith as a grain of mustard seed, I can say to a mountain, "Move," and it will move and *nothing* will be impossible to me. I'm a believer; I'm not a doubter. I know that without faith it is impossible to please God. I know I am to live by faith, and if I shrink back, the Lord has no pleasure in me.

Every man is given a measure of faith; I'll develop my faith to the glory of God. I have faith toward God. My faith is not in my faith, but in a living God who said He would never fail or forsake me. Therefore I choose to walk by faith and not by sight. I trust in the Lord with all my heart and don't lean to my own understanding. I'm not ruled by my feelings, I'm not in bondage to my emotions. I'm not under the circumstances; I'm above the circumstances. I'm seated with Christ in heavenly places. The steps of a righteous man are ordered by the Lord. Many are the afflictions of the righteous, but the Lord delivers them out of them all.

The righteous man falls seven times but rises again. Champions don't give up, they get up. One thing I do, forgetting what lies behind, straining forward to what lies ahead, I press on toward the goal for the prize of the upward call of God in Christ Jesus, my Lord. I put my hand to the plow and I don't look back. I run to win. Zeal for Your house consumes me. The kingdom of heaven comes by violence, and those who take it, take it by force.

It's not by might, nor by power, but by His Spirit. He ever lives to make intercession for me. He is able to do exceedingly far more abundantly above all that I ever dare think or ask, by the power at work within me. He who began a good work in me will bring it to completion in the day of the Lord Jesus.

Boldly, I can approach the throne of grace to receive mercy and grace for help in the time of need. I'll be anxious for nothing. He will keep me in perfect peace for my mind is stayed on Him. Therefore I enter His rest. I've been crucified with Christ, nevertheless I live; and the life I now live, I live by faith in the Son of God who loved me and gave Himself for me.

Whatever is borne of God overcomes the world. This is the victory that overcomes the world, even my faith. I choose this day to live by faith, to walk by faith, to see throught the eye of faith. Therefore, I am an overcomer. I'm going from faith to faith, and I'll see through the eye of faith. Therefore, I am an overcomer. I'm going from faith to faith, strength to strength, glory to glory. The path of the righteous is like the light of dawn which shines brighter until full day!

BOLDNESS

I give no opportunity to the devil. I give no place to fear in my life. That which man fears comes upon him. Fear has torment. The fear of man brings a snare, but perfect love casts out fear. I sought the Lord and He heard me and delivered me from all my fears. God has not given me a spirit of fear, but a spirit of love, power and a sound mind. In righteousness I am established, so I'll be far from oppression. I will not fear or be in terror. It shall not come near me. The Lord is my light and my salvation. Whom shall I fear? The Lord is the strength of my life; of whom shall I be afraid? God is my refuge and my strength, a very present help in trouble. Therefore I will not fear. If I were still trying to please men, I should not be a servant of Jesus Christ. But I am a servant of the Most High God. I fear not, for He is with me. I'll not be dismayed, for He is my God. He will strengthen me; He will help me; He will uphold me with His victorious right hand.

I'm not ashamed of the gospel for it is power of God unto salvation to those who believe. I'm a minister of reconciliation. I'm an ambassador for Jesus Christ. The anointing breaks every yoke. I received power when the Holy Spirit came upon me to be His witness. His Word, which comes out of His mouth, will not return void but will accomplish His purpose and prosper in the thing for which it was sent. I know my God; I am strong; I will do exploits. As He is, so am I in this world.

I am righteous; therefore, I am bold as a lion. He will never fail me or forsake me; therefore, I can say boldly, "The Lord is my helper; I'll not be afraid. What can man do to me?" As a young man, I am strong. The Word of God abides in me. I have overcome the evil one. I am an overcomer. Greater is He that is in me than he that is in the world. I am a hundredfold Christian. I am complete in Him. I am more than a conqueror through Christ who loves me. Grant, Lord, to Your servant to speak Your Word with all boldness while You stretch out Your hand to heal and signs and wonders are performed through the name of Your holy servant, Jesus!

HEALTH

I will bless my Lord with all my heart, for He not only forgives all my sins, He heals all my diseases. Because the Lord is my refuge, the most High my habitation, no evil shall befall me, no plague will come near my dwelling place. He gives His angels charge over me to guard me in all my ways.

It's His will that I prosper and be in health, even as my soul does prosper. Jesus of Nazareth went about doing good and healing all who were oppressed of the devil. He said, "I'll remove sickness from the midst of you." He is the Lord, my healer. I look not to the healing, but to the Healer—Jesus, my loving Lord. My body is for the Lord and the Lord is for my body. He bore away my sickness and carried away my diseases and by His stripes, I was healed.

The Son of Righteousness shall rise with healing in His wings. The same Spirit that raised Jesus from the dead is at work in my mortal body, giving me life. I expect a miracle. Jesus Christ is the same yesterday, today and forever. Is anything too hard for the Lord? For all things are possible to him who believes. I'm not just a hearer of the Word, I'm a doer of the Word. Therefore, I am blessed in my doing, for faith without action is dead. It is done unto me according to my faith. Therefore, I will not only confess the Word, but I will be a doer of the Word!

JOY

I renounce a spirit of heaviness and put on the garment of praise so that He may be glorified. I will bless the Lord at all times. His praise will continually be in my mouth. The joy of the Lord is my strength. Jesus bore my grief.

This is the day that the Lord has made; I will rejoice and be glad in it. I rejoice with joy unspeakable and full of glory. I rejoice in the Lord always. I do all things without grumbling and complaining. His words were found and I ate them, and they became unto me a joy and a delight to my heart. In spite of trials, I offer sacrifices of joy. I will sing; yes, I will sing praises unto the Lord. I have the high praises of God in my throat and a two-edge sword in my hand.

I have set the Lord always before me. Because He is at my right, I shall not be moved. Therefore, my heart is glad and my soul rejoices. My body also dwells secure. You will show me the path of life. In Your presence there is fullness of joy. At Your right hand are pleasures forevermore. I will rejoice in the Lord; I will rejoice in the God of my salvation.

I wait upon the Lord and He renews my strength. I will mount up with wings like eagles. I will run and not be weary; I will walk and not faint.

PROSPERITY

I continue to keep my way of life free from the love of money. I cannot serve God and money. All things come from You, and of Your own I have given You. Being faithful with money, I am entrusted with true riches. I do not rob God in my tithes and offerings; therefore, I'm not cursed with a curse and the devourer is rebuked. I put the Lord to the test and the Lord opens the windows of heaven and pours down an overwhelming blessing.

I do not grow weary in doing good, for in due season I reap because I do not lose heart. I cast my bread upon the waters and I find it after many days. One man gives freely yet grows all the richer; another withholds what he should give and only suffers want. The generous man will be enriched and one who waters will himself be watered.

I've been young and now am old; yet, I've not seen the righteous forsaken or his children begging bread. I am ever giving liberally and lending, and my children became a blessing. My God supplies all my needs according to His riches in glory in Christ Jesus. I give and it is given to me; good measure, pressed down, shaken together, running over, men give into my bosom. If I sow sparingly, then I will also reap sparingly. So I will sow bountifully and, therefore, reap bountifully. God loves a cheerful giver.

He is able to provide me with every blessing in abundance, so I may always have enough of everything in order to provide in abundance for every good work. He who supplies seed to the sower and bread for food will supply and multiply my resources and increase the harvest of my righteousness.

I do not sell godliness as a means of selfish gain. My passion is to see the gospel of the Kingdom preached throughout the whole world as a testimony to all the nations, so then the end will come. I do all I can to hasten the coming of that day!

DESTINY

The eyes of the Lord run to and fro throughout the whole earth in order to show Himself strong in behalf of those whose hearts are fully blameless toward Him. God rewards those who diligently seek Him. He who calls me is faithful and He will do it.

I'm not lukewarm. I'm not a compromiser. I'll not be conformed to the world. I'm not a loser; I'm a winner. I'm a partaker of His divine nature. God indwells my body. I run the race to win. His grace is sufficient for me. His power is made perfect in weakness.

When the enemy comes in like a flood, the Spirit of the Lord will raise up a standard. I'm part of that standard. We are the soldiers of the army of salvation that God is raising up to save this world. I'll not despise the day of small beginnings. We will reclaim that which the thief has stolen through tradition and ignorance. The earth is the Lord's and the fullness thereof, the world and all who dwell therein. He said He would pour out His Spirit in these last days. Sons and daughters would prophesy; young men would see visions; old men would dream dreams. I'm part of this end-time vision, for without it, I will perish. For still the vision awaits its appointed time. It hastens to the end; it will not fail. If it seems slow, I will wait for it. It will surely come. It will not delay. Therefore, I have a sense of destiny. Jesus is restoring His Church; He is coming back for a glorious Church without spot or wrinkle or blemish or any such thing. It will be a triumphant Church. It will kick in the gates of hell. I'm a part of this end-time move.

I'll pay the price. I'm giving my utmost for His highest. I press on toward the goal for the prize of the high call of God in Christ Jesus, my Lord. I'm out to change my generation. I'm beginning today. I redeem the time. I'm not weighed down by the cares of this life. I cast my cares on the Lord.

Whatever the task this day, I'll do it heartily as serving the Lord. I'll pursue excellence, for I serve the God of excellence. I'll stir up the gifts within me. I'll step out in faith. I'll move in the supernatural. I'll set the captives free.

The Spirit of the Lord is upon me. He has anointed me to preach the good news to the poor. He has sent me to proclaim release to the captives, recovery of sight to the blind, to set at liberty those who are oppressed, to bind up the brokenhearted and to proclaim the acceptable year of the Lord.

I'll not limit the Holy One of Israel. I'll not be disobedient to the heavenly vision. The kingdoms of this world shall become the kingdoms of our God and of His Christ!

Now to Him Who is able to keep me from falling and to present me without blemish before the presence of His glory with exceeding joy, to the only God, my Savior, through Jesus Christ my Lord, be glory, majesty, dominion and authority before time and now forever! Amen![1]

Note

1. Larry Tomczak, "Biblical Declarations to Build Strong Faith." Reprinted with permission. The content of these declarations is almost completely the Word of God. Scripture references are not included in order to save space. If you are interested in finding the references, you can derive them from a Bible concordance.

Appendix C

RECOMMENDED READING

Ahn, Ché. *The Authority of the Believer and Healing.* Colorado Springs, CO: Wagner Publications, 1999.

———. *Into the Fire.* Ventura, CA: Renew Books, 1998.

Ahn, Ché, ed. *Hosting the Holy Spirit.* Ventura, CA: Renew Books, 2000.

Bosworth, F. F. *Christ the Healer.* Grand Rapids, MI: Fleming H. Revell, 2000.

Deere, Jack. *Surprised by the Voice of God.* Grand Rapids, MI: Zondervan Publishing House, 1998.

Harding, Ed. *What Christians Should Know About Sickness and Healing.* Tonbridge, England: Sovereign World Limited, 1997.

Hinn, Benny. *The Anointing.* Nashville, TN: Thomas Nelson, 1992.

———. *Good Morning, Holy Spirit.* Nashville, TN: Thomas Nelson, 1997.

Jacobs, Cindy. *Deliver Us from Evil.* Ventura, CA: Regal Books, 2001.

———. *Possessing the Gates of the Enemy.* Shippensburg, PA: Destiny Image, 1994.

———. *The Voice of God.* Ventura, CA: Regal Books, 1995.

Kraft, Charles H. *Deep Wounds, Deep Healing.* Ann Arbor, MI: Vine Books, 1993.

Kuhlman, Kathryn, and Jamie Buckingham. *Daughter of Destiny.* North Brunswick, NJ: Bridge-Logos Publishers, 1999.

Kydd, Ronald A. N. *Healing Through the Centuries*. Peabody, MA: Hendrickson Publishers, 1998.

MacNutt, Francis. *Healing*. Notre Dame, IN: Ave Maria Press, 1999.

Osteen, Dodie. *Healed of Cancer*. Houston, TX: John Osteen Publications, 1986.

Pierce, Chuck D., with John Dickson, *The Worship Warrior*. Ventura, CA: Regal Books, 2002.

Pierce, Chuck D., and Rebecca Wagner Sytsema. *When God Speaks*. Colorado Springs, CO: Wagner Publications, 2003.

Rumph, Jane. *Signs and Wonders in America Today*. Ann Arbor, MI: Vine Books, 2003.

Wagner, C. Peter. *Acts of the Holy Spirit*. Ventura, CA: Regal Books, 2000.

——. *How to Have a Healing Ministry Without Making Your Church Sick!* Ventura, CA: Regal Books, 1988.

Warner, Wayne E. *Kathryn Kuhlman: The Woman Behind the Miracles*. Ann Arbor, MI: Vine Books, 1993.

Wimber, John, with Kevin Springer. *Power Healing*. San Francisco: Harper and Row Publishers, 1987.

FOR MORE INFORMATION OR TO CONTACT THE AUTHOR:

Harvest Rock Church
626-794-1199
website: www.harvestrockchurch.org
e-mail: info@harvestrockchurch.org

Harvest International Ministries
626-720-8154
e-mail: himintl@aol.com

Also from Ché Ahn

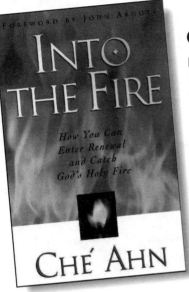

Catch Revival Fire!

Into the Fire
How You Can Enter Renewal
and Catch God's Holy Fire

Trade Paper • ISBN 08307.21495

This is Ché Ahn's inspiring story of his journey
from survival to revival—a journey that birthed
a new church, a new movement, a renewed
marriage and a consuming passion for Jesus.
Discover how you, too, can enter renewal and
fan the flames of revival within yourself, your
family and your church!

Moving from Visitation to Habitation

Hosting the Holy Spirit
Inviting the Holy Spirit to Abide with You

Trade Paper • ISBN 08307.25849

Why do we experience God's presence in some
places more than others? Because the Holy Spirit
is welcomed, appreciated and honored in these
churches and thus delights in abiding there—
not merely as a guest lecturer, but as the Spirit
of the King of glory who dwells there. The difference between *visitation* and *habitation* is revealed
and shared by those who have experienced
the movement of God around the world:
Ché Ahn, John Arnott, Frank Damazio, Lou Engle,
Kingsley Fletcher, Cindy Jacobs, John Kilpatrick,
Bart Pierce, Winkie Pratney, Sergio Scataglini,
Wendell Smith and Tommy Tenney. The Holy
Spirit wants to abide, remain and grow with
you. Open your door to His enduring grace.

Pick up a copy at your favorite Christian bookstore!
www.regalbooks.com

Regal
God's Word for Your World™

Tap into the Power of Prayer

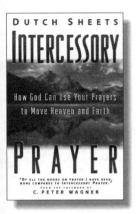

Intercessory Prayer
How God Can Use Your Prayers
to Move Heaven and Earth
Dutch Sheets
Trade Paper • 275p
ISBN 08307.19008

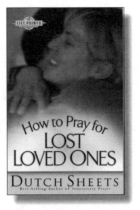

**How to Pray for Lost
Loved Ones**
Our designated role of reaching
our lost loved ones for God
Dutch Sheets
Trade Paper • 112p
ISBN 08307.27655

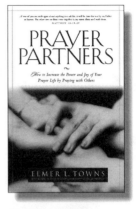

Prayer Partners
How to Increase the Power and
Joy of Your Prayer Life by Praying
with Others
Elmer Towns
Trade Paper • 120p
ISBN 08307.29348

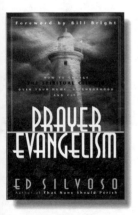

Prayer Evangelism
How to Change the Spiritual
Climate over Your Home,
Neighborhood and City
Ed Silvoso
Trade Paper • 256p
ISBN 08307.23978

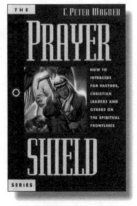

Prayer Shield
How to Intercede for Pastors,
Christian Leaders and Others
in the Spiritual Frontlines
C. Peter Wagner
Trade Paper • 208p
ISBN 08307.15142

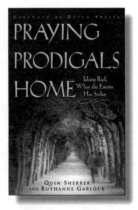

Praying Prodigals Home
Taking Back What the
Enemy Has Stolen
Quin Sherrer and *Ruthanne Garlock*
Trade Paper • 238p
ISBN 08307.25636

Pick up a copy at your favorite Christian bookstore!
www.regalbooks.com

God's Word for Your World™